WORKERS OF ALL COUNTRIES, UNITE!

V. I. LENIN

"LEFT-WING" COMMUNISM, AN INFANTILE DISORDER

FOREIGN LANGUAGES PRESS
PEKING 1970

First Edition 1965
Second Printing 1970

PUBLISHER'S NOTE

The present English translation of V. I. Lenin's *"Left-Wing" Communism, an Infantile Disorder* is a reprint of the text given in V. I. Lenin, *Selected Works,* English edition, Foreign Languages Publishing House, Moscow, 1952, Vol. II, Part 2. The notes at the end of the book are based on those given in the English edition and in the Chinese edition published by the People's Publishing House, Peking, in September 1964.

Printed in the People's Republic of China

CONTENTS

"LEFT-WING" COMMUNISM, AN INFANTILE DISORDER[1]

I

IN WHAT SENSE CAN WE SPEAK OF THE INTERNATIONAL SIGNIFICANCE OF THE RUSSIAN REVOLUTION?

In the first months following the conquest of political power by the proletariat in Russia (October 25 [November 7], 1917), it might have seemed that the tremendous difference between backward Russia and the advanced countries of Western Europe would cause the proletarian revolution in these latter countries to have very little resemblance to ours. Now we already have very considerable international experience which most definitely shows that certain fundamental features of our revolution have a significance which is not local, not peculiarly national, not Russian only, but international. I speak here of international significance not in the broad sense of the term: not some, but all the fundamental and many of the secondary features of our revolution are of international significance in the sense that the revolution influences all countries. No, taking it in the narrowest sense, i.e., understanding international significance to mean the international validity or the historical inevitability of a repetition on an international scale of what has taken place in our country, it must be admitted that certain fundamental features of our revolution do possess such a significance.

Of course, it would be a very great mistake to exaggerate this truth and to apply it not only to certain fundamental features of our revolution. It would also be a mistake to lose sight of the fact that after the victory of the proletarian revolution in at least one of the advanced countries things will in all probability take a sharp turn, viz., Russia will soon after cease to be the model country and once again become a backward country (in the "Soviet" and the socialist sense).

But at the present moment of history the situation is precisely such that the Russian model reveals to *all* countries something, and something very essential, of their near and inevitable future. Advanced workers in every land have long understood this; and more often they have not so much understood it as grasped it, sensed it, by revolutionary class instinct. Herein lies the international "significance" (in the narrow sense of the term) of Soviet power, and of the fundamentals of Bolshevik theory and tactics. This the "revolutionary" leaders of the Second International, such as Kautsky in Germany and Otto Bauer and Friedrich Adler in Austria, failed to understand, and therefore proved to be reactionaries and advocates of the worst kind of opportunism and social treachery. Incidentally, the anonymous pamphlet entitled *The World Revolution* ("Weltrevolution") which appeared in 1919 in Vienna (Sozialistische Bücherei, Heft 11; Ignaz Brand) very clearly reveals their whole process of

2

thought and their whole circle of ideas, or, rather, the full depth of their stupidity, pedantry, baseness and betrayal of working-class interests — and, moreover, under the guise of "defending" the idea of "world revolution."

But we shall have to discuss this pamphlet in greater detail some other time. Here we shall note only one more point: long, long ago, Kautsky, when he was still a Marxist and not a renegade, approaching the question as a historian, foresaw the possibility of a situation arising in which the revolutionary spirit of the Russian proletariat would serve as a model for Western Europe. This was in 1902, when Kautsky wrote an article for the revolutionary *Iskra* entitled "The Slavs and Revolution." This is what he wrote in the article:

"At the present time" (in contrast to 1848) "it would seem that not only have the Slavs entered the ranks of the revolutionary nations, but that the centre of revolutionary thought and revolutionary action is shifting more and more to the Slavs. The revolutionary centre is shifting from the West to the East. In the first half of the nineteenth century it was in France, at times in England. In 1848 Germany joined the ranks of the revolutionary nations. . . . The new century opens with events which suggest the thought that we are approaching a further shift of the revolutionary centre, namely, to Russia. . . . Russia, which has borrowed so much revolutionary initiative from the West, is now perhaps herself ready to serve as a source of revolutionary energy for the West. The Russian revolutionary movement that is now flaring up will perhaps prove to be the most potent means of exorcising that spirit of flabby philistinism and temperate politics which is beginning to spread in our midst, and it may cause the thirst for battle and the passionate devotion to our great ideals to flare up in bright flames again. Russia has long ceased to be merely a bulwark of reaction and absolutism for Western Europe. It might be said that today the very opposite is the case. Western Europe is becoming a bulwark of reaction and absolutism in Russia. . . . The Russian revolutionaries might perhaps have coped with the tsar long ago had they not been compelled at the same time to fight his ally, European capital. Let us hope that this time they will succeed in coping with both enemies, and that the new 'Holy Alliance' will collapse more quickly than its predecessors. But however the present struggle in Russia may end, the blood and felicity of the martyrs, whom, unfortunately, it will produce in too great numbers, will not have been sacrificed in vain. They will nourish the shoots of social revolution throughout the civilized world and make them grow more luxuriantly and rapidly. In 1848 the Slavs were a black frost which blighted the flowers of the people's spring. Perhaps they are now destined to be the storm that will break the ice of reaction and irresistibly bring with it a new and happy spring for the nations." (Karl Kautsky, "The Slavs and Revolution," *Iskra*, Russian Social-Democratic revolutionary newspaper, No. 18, March 10, 1902.)

Karl Kautsky wrote well eighteen years ago!

II

ONE OF THE FUNDAMENTAL CONDITIONS
FOR THE BOLSHEVIKS' SUCCESS

Certainly, almost everyone now realizes that the Bolsheviks could not have maintained themselves in power for two and a half months, let alone two and a half years, unless the strictest, truly iron discipline had prevailed in our Party, and unless the latter had been rendered the fullest and unreserved support of the whole mass of the working class, that is, of all its thinking, honest, self-sacrificing and influential elements who are capable of leading or of carrying with them the backward strata.

The dictatorship of the proletariat is a most determined and most ruthless war waged by the new class against a *more powerful* enemy, the bourgeoisie, whose resistance is increased *tenfold* by its overthrow (even if only in one country), and whose power lies not only in the strength of international capital, in the strength and durability of the international connections of the bourgeoisie, but also in the *force of habit*, in the strength of *small production*. For, unfortunately, small production is still very, very widespread in the world, and small production *engenders* capitalism and the bourgeoisie continuously, daily, hourly, spontaneously, and on a mass scale. For all these reasons the dictatorship of the proletariat is essential, and victory over the bourgeoisie is impossible without a long, stubborn and desperate war of life and death, a war demanding perseverance, discipline, firmness, indomitableness and unity of will.

I repeat, the experience of the victorious dictatorship of the proletariat in Russia has clearly shown even to those who are unable to think, or who have not had occasion to ponder over this question, that absolute centralization and the strictest discipline of the proletariat constitute one of the fundamental conditions for victory over the bourgeoisie.

This is often discussed. But not nearly enough thought is given to what it means, and under what conditions it is possible. Would it not be better if greetings in honour of Soviet power and the Bolsheviks were *more frequently* attended by a *profound analysis* of the reasons *why* the Bolsheviks were able to build up the discipline the revolutionary proletariat needs?

As a trend of political thought and as a political party, Bolshevism exists since 1903. Only the history of Bolshevism during the *whole* period of its existence can satisfactorily explain why it was able to build up and to maintain under most difficult conditions the iron discipline needed for the victory of the proletariat.

And first of all the question arises: how is the discipline of the revolutionary party of the proletariat maintained? How is it tested? How is it reinforced? First, by the class consciousness of the proletarian vanguard and by its devotion to the revolution, by its perseverance, self-sacrifice and heroism. Secondly, by its ability to link itself with, to keep in close

6

touch with, and to a certain extent, if you like, to merge with the broadest masses of the toilers — primarily with the proletariat, *but also with the non-proletarian* toiling masses. Thirdly, by the correctness of the political leadership exercised by this vanguard, by the correctness of its political strategy and tactics, provided that the broadest masses have been convinced *by their own experience* that they are correct. Without these conditions, discipline in a revolutionary party that is really capable of being the party of the advanced class, whose mission it is to overthrow the bourgeoisie and transform the whole of society, cannot be achieved. Without these conditions, all attempts to establish discipline inevitably fall flat and end in phrase-mongering and grimacing. On the other hand, these conditions cannot arise all at once. They are created only by prolonged effort and hard-won experience. Their creation is facilitated by correct revolutionary theory, which, in its turn, is not a dogma, but assumes final shape only in close connection with the practical activity of a truly mass and truly revolutionary movement.

That Bolshevism was able, in 1917-20, under unprecedentedly difficult conditions, to build up and successfully maintain the strictest centralization and iron discipline was simply due to a number of historical peculiarities of Russia.

On the one hand, Bolshevism arose in 1903 on the very firm foundation of the theory of Marxism. And the correctness of this — and only this — revolutionary theory has been proved not only by world experience throughout the nineteenth century, but particularly by the experience of the wanderings and vacillations, the mistakes and disappointments of revolutionary thought in Russia. For nearly half a century — approximately from the forties to the nineties — advanced thought in Russia, oppressed by an unparalleled, savage and reactionary tsardom, eagerly sought for a correct revolutionary theory and followed with astonishing diligence and thoroughness each and every "last word" in this realm in Europe and America. Russia achieved Marxism, the only correct revolutionary theory, through veritable *suffering*, through half a century of unprecedented torment and sacrifice, of unprecedented revolutionary heroism, incredible energy, devoted searching, study, practical trial, disappointment, verification and comparison with European experience. Thanks to the enforced emigration caused by tsardom, revolutionary Russia in the second half of the nineteenth century possessed such a wealth of international connections and such excellent information on world forms and theories of the revolutionary movement as no other country in the world.

On the other hand, having arisen on this granite theoretical foundation, Bolshevism passed through fifteen years (1903-17) of practical history which in wealth of experience has no equal anywhere else in the world. For no other country during these fifteen years had anything even approximating to this revolutionary experience, this rapid and varied succession of different forms of the movement — legal and illegal, peaceful and stormy, underground and open, circles and mass movements, parliamentary and terrorist. In no other country was there concentrated during so short a time such a wealth of forms, shades, and methods of struggle of *all* classes of modern society, and moreover, a struggle which, owing to the backwardness of the country and the severity of the tsarist yoke, matured with exceptional rapidity and assimilated most eagerly and successfully the appropriate "last word" of American and European political experience.

III

THE PRINCIPAL STAGES IN THE HISTORY OF BOLSHEVISM

The years of preparation of the revolution (1903-05). The approach of a great storm is felt everywhere. All classes are in a state of ferment and preparation. Abroad, the press of the political exiles discusses the theoretical aspects of *all* the fundamental problems of the revolution. The representatives of the three main classes, of the three principal political trends, the liberal-bourgeois, the petty bourgeois-democratic (concealed under the labels "social-democratic" and "social-revolutionary"), and the proletarian-revolutionary trends, anticipate and prepare the approaching open class struggle by a most bitter battle on programmatical and tactical views. *All* the issues on which the masses waged an armed struggle in 1905-07 and 1917-20 can (and should) be studied in their embryonic form in the press of that time. Between these three main trends, there were, of course, a host of intermediate, transitional, halfway forms. Or, more correctly, in the struggle of the press, parties, factions and groups, there were crystallizing those political and ideological trends which

9

are actually class trends; the classes were forging the requisite political and ideological weapons for the impending battles.

The years of revolution (1905-07). All classes come out into the open. All programmatical and tactical views are tested by the action of the masses. The strike struggle is unparalleled anywhere in the world for its extent and acuteness. The economic strike grows into a political strike, and the latter into insurrection. The relations between the proletariat, as the leader, and the vacillating, unstable peasantry, as the led, are tested in practice. The Soviet form of organization is born in the spontaneous development of the struggle. The controversies of that time over the significance of the Soviets anticipate the great struggle of 1917-20. The alternation of parliamentary and non-parliamentary forms of struggle, of tactics of boycotting parliament and tactics of participating in parliament, of legal and illegal forms of struggle, and likewise their interrelations and connections— all of this is distinguished by an astonishing richness of content. As far as teaching the fundamentals of political science — to masses and leaders, to classes and parties — was concerned, one month of this period was equivalent to a whole year of "peaceful," "constitutional" development. Without the "dress rehearsal" of 1905, the victory of the October Revolution in 1917 would have been impossible.

The years of reaction (1907-10). Tsardom scored victory. All the revolutionary and opposition parties have been defeated. Depression, demoralization, splits, discord, renegacy, pornography take the place of politics. There is an increased drift toward philosophical idealism; mysticism becomes the shell of counter-revolutionary sentiments. But at the same time, it is precisely this great defeat that gives the revolutionary parties and the revolutionary class a real and very valuable lesson, a lesson in historical dialectics, a lesson in the understanding of the political struggle and in the skill and art of waging it. One gets to know one's friends in times of misfortune. Defeated armies learn well.

Victorious tsardom is compelled to accelerate the destruction of the remnants of the prebourgeois, patriarchal mode of life in Russia. The country's development along bourgeois lines proceeds with remarkable speed. Extra-class and above-class illusions, illusions concerning the possibility of avoiding capitalism, are scattered to the winds. The class struggle manifests itself in quite a new and more distinct form.

The revolutionary parties must complete their education. They have learned to attack. Now they have to realize that this knowledge must be supplemented with the knowledge how to retreat properly. They have to realize — and the revolutionary class is taught to realize it by its own bitter experience — that victory is impossible unless they have learned both how to attack and how to retreat properly. Of all the defeated opposition and revolutionary parties, the Bolsheviks effected the most orderly retreat, with the least loss to their "army," with its core best preserved, with the least (in respect to profundity and irremediability) splits, with the least demoralization, and in the best condition to resume the work on the broadest scale and in the most correct and energetic manner. The Bolsheviks achieved this only because they ruthlessly exposed and expelled the revolutionary phrase-mongers, who refused to understand that one had to retreat, that one had to know how to retreat, and that one had absolutely to learn how to work legally in the most reactionary parliaments, in the most reactionary trade unions, cooperative societies, insurance societies and similar organizations.

The years of rise (1910-14). At first the rise was incredibly slow; then, following the Lena events of 1912,[2] it became somewhat more rapid. Overcoming unprecedented difficulties, the Bolsheviks pushed aside the Mensheviks, whose role as agents of the bourgeoisie in the working-class movement was perfectly understood by the whole bourgeoisie after 1905, and who were therefore supported in a thousand ways by the whole bourgeoisie against the Bolsheviks. But the Bolsheviks would never have succeeded in doing this had they not carried out a correct tactic of combining illegal work with the obligatory utilization of "legal possibilities." The Bolsheviks won all the labour seats in the arch-reactionary Duma.

The first imperialist world war (1914-17). Legal parliamentarism, with an extremely reactionary "parliament," is of very useful service to the party of the revolutionary proletariat, the Bolsheviks. The Bolshevik deputies are exiled to Siberia. In the exile press abroad all shades of social-imperialism, social-chauvinism, social-patriotism, inconsistent and consistent internationalism, pacifism, and the revolutionary repudiation of pacifist illusions find full expression. The learned fools and old women of the Second International, who had arrogantly and contemptuously turned up their noses at the abundance of "factions" in the Russian socialist movement and at the bitter struggle they waged among themselves, were unable — when the war deprived them of their vaunted "legality" in *all* the advanced countries — to organize anything even approximating such a free (illegal) interchange of views and such a free (illegal) working out of correct views as the Russian revolutionaries did in Switzerland and in a number of other countries. It was precisely because of this that both the avowed social-patriots and the "Kautskyites" of all countries proved to be the worst traitors to the proletariat. And one of the principal reasons why Bolshevism was able to score victory in 1917-20 was that ever since the end of 1914 it had been ruthlessly exposing the baseness, loathsomeness and vileness of social-chauvinism and "Kautskyism" (to which Longuetism[3] in France, the views of the leaders of the Independent Labour Party[4] and the Fabians[5] in England, of Turati in Italy, etc., correspond), and the masses later became more and more convinced by their own experience of the correctness of the Bolshevik views.

The second revolution in Russia (February to October 1917). The incredible senility and obsoleteness of tsardom had created (with the aid of the blows and hardships of a most agonizing war) an incredibly destructive power directed against tsardom. Within a few days Russia was transformed into a democratic bourgeois republic, more free — under war conditions — than any other country in the world. The leaders of the opposition and revolutionary parties began to set up a government, just as is done in the most "strictly parliamentary" republics; and the fact that a man had been a leader of an opposition party in parliament, even in a most reactionary parliament, *assisted* him in his subsequent role in the revolution.

In a few weeks the Mensheviks and "Socialist-Revolutionaries" thoroughly imbibed all the methods and manners, arguments and sophistries of the European heroes of the Second International, of the ministerialists and other opportunist scum. All that we now read about the Scheidemanns and Noskes, about Kautsky and Hilferding, Renner and Austerlitz, Otto Bauer and Fritz Adler, Turati and Longuet, about the Fabians and the leaders of the Independent Labour

13

Party of England — all this seems to us (and really is) a dreary repetition, a reiteration of an old and familiar refrain. We have already seen all this in the case of the Mensheviks. History played a joke and made the opportunists of a backward country anticipate the opportunists of a number of advanced countries.

If the heroes of the Second International have all suffered bankruptcy and have disgraced themselves over the question of the significance and role of the Soviets and Soviet power; if the leaders of the three very important parties which have now left the Second International (namely, the German Independent Social-Democratic Party,[6] the French Longuetites and the British Independent Labour Party) have disgraced and entangled themselves over this question in a most "striking" way; if they have all turned out to be slaves to the prejudices of petty-bourgeois democracy (quite in the spirit of the petty bourgeois of 1848 who called themselves "Social-Democrats") — we have *already* seen *all this* in the case of the Mensheviks. History played a joke: in Russia, in 1905, the Soviets were born, from February to October 1917 they were turned to a false use by the Mensheviks, who went bankrupt because of their inability to understand the role and significance of the Soviets; and now the idea of Soviet power has arisen *all over the world* and is spreading among the proletariat of all countries with extraordinary speed. And the old heroes of the Second International are also going bankrupt *everywhere,* like our Mensheviks, because they are not capable of understanding the role and significance of the Soviets. Experience has proved that on certain very essential questions of the proletarian revolution, *all* countries will inevitably have to perform what Russia has performed.

14

Contrary to the views that are today not infrequently met with in Europe and America, the Bolsheviks began their victorious struggle against the parliamentary (factually) bourgeois republic and against the Mensheviks very cautiously, and the preparations they made for it were by no means simple. We did *not* call for the overthrow of the government at the beginning of the period mentioned, but explained that it was impossible to overthrow it *without* first changing the composition and the sentiments of the Soviets. We did not proclaim a boycott of the bourgeois parliament, the Constituent Assembly, but said — and from the April (1917) Conference of our Party onwards began to say officially in the name of the Party — that a bourgeois republic with a Constituent Assembly is better than a bourgeois republic without a Constituent Assembly, but that a "workers' and peasants' " republic, a Soviet republic, is better than any bourgeois-democratic, parliamentary, republic. Without such careful, thorough, circumspect and prolonged preparations we could not have obtained victory in October 1917, nor have maintained that victory.

IV

IN THE STRUGGLE AGAINST WHAT
ENEMIES WITHIN THE WORKING-CLASS
MOVEMENT DID BOLSHEVISM GROW UP
AND BECOME STRONG AND STEELED?

Firstly and principally, in the struggle against opportunism, which in 1914 had definitely grown into social-chauvinism, had definitely sided with the bourgeoisie against the proletariat. Naturally, this was the principal enemy of Bolshevism within the working-class movement. It remains the principal enemy internationally too. The Bolsheviks devoted, and continue to devote, most attention to this enemy. This aspect of Bolshevik activities is now fairly well known abroad too.

Something different, however, must be said of the other enemy of Bolshevism within the working-class movement. It is far from sufficiently known as yet abroad that Bolshevism grew up, took shape, and became steeled in long years of struggle against *petty-bourgeois revolutionism*, which smacks of, or borrows something from, anarchism, and which falls short, in anything essential, of the conditions and requirements of a consistently proletarian class struggle. For Marxists, it is well established theoretically — and the experience of all European revolutions and revolutionary movements has fully confirmed it — that the small owner, the small master (a social type that is represented in many European countries on a very wide, a mass scale), who under capitalism always suffers oppression and, very often, an incredibly acute and rapid deterioration in his conditions, and ruin, easily goes to revolutionary extremes, but is incapable of perseverance, organization, discipline and steadfastness. The petty bourgeois "driven to frenzy" by the horrors of capitalism is a social phenomenon which, like anarchism, is characteristic of all capitalist countries. The instability of such revolutionism, its barrenness, its liability to become swiftly transformed into submission, apathy, fantasy, and even a "frenzied" infatuation with one or another bourgeois "fad" — all this is a matter of common knowledge. But a theoretical, abstract recognition of these truths does not at all free revolutionary parties from old mistakes, which always crop up at unexpected moments, in a somewhat new form, in hitherto unknown vestments or surroundings, in a peculiar — more or less peculiar — situation.

Anarchism was not infrequently a sort of punishment for the opportunist sins of the working-class movement. The two monstrosities were mutually complementary. And the fact that in Russia, although her population is more petty bourgeois than that of the European countries, anarchism exercised a relatively negligible influence in the preparations for and during both revolutions (1905 and 1917), must undoubtedly be partly placed to the credit of Bolshevism, which has always combated opportunism ruthlessly and uncompromisingly. I say "partly," for a still more important role in weakening the influence of anarchism in Russia was played by the fact that in the past (in the seventies of the nineteenth century) it had had the opportunity to develop with exceptional luxuriance and to display its utter fallaciousness and unfitness as a guiding theory for the revolutionary class.

At its inception in 1903, Bolshevism took over the tradition of ruthless struggle against petty-bourgeois, semianarchist (or dilettante-anarchist) revolutionism, the tradition which has always existed in revolutionary Social-Democracy, and became particularly strong in 1900-03, when the foundations for a mass party of the revolutionary proletariat were being laid in Russia. Bolshevism took over and continued the struggle against the party which more than any other expressed the tendencies of petty-bourgeois revolutionism, namely, the "Socialist-Revolutionary" Party, and waged this struggle on three main points. First, this party, rejecting Marxism, stubbornly refused (or, it would be more correct to say: was unable) to understand the need for a strictly objective appraisal of the class forces and their interrelations before undertaking any political action. Secondly, this party considered itself to be particularly "revolutionary," or "Left," because of its recognition of individual terror, assassination — a thing which we Marxists emphatically rejected. Of course, we rejected individual terror only on grounds of expediency, whereas people who were capable of condemning "on principle" the terror of the Great French Revolution, or in general, the terror employed by a victorious revolutionary party which is besieged by the bourgeoisie of the whole world, were ridiculed and laughed to scorn already by Plekhanov, in 1900-03, when he was a Marxist and a revolutionary. Thirdly, the "Socialist-Revolutionaries" thought it very "Left" to sneer at comparatively insignificant opportunist sins of the German Social-Democratic Party, while they themselves imitated the extreme opportunists of that party, for example, on the agrarian question, or on the question of the dictatorship of the proletariat.

History, by the way, has now confirmed on a large, world-wide historic scale the opinion we have always advocated, namely, that *revolutionary* German Social-Democracy (note that as far back as 1900-03 Plekhanov demanded the expulsion of Bernstein from the party, and the Bolsheviks, always continuing this tradition, in 1913 exposed the utter baseness, vileness and treachery of Legien[7]) *came closest* to being the party which the revolutionary proletariat required in order to attain victory. Now, in 1920, after all the ignominious failures and crises of the war period and the early postwar years, it can be plainly seen that, of all the Western parties, German revolutionary Social-Democracy produced the best leaders, and recovered, recuperated, and gained new strength more rapidly than the others. This may be seen in the case both of the Spartacist party[8] and the Left, proletarian wing of the "Independent Social-Democratic Party of Germany," which is waging an incessant struggle against the opportunism and spinelessness of the Kautskys, Hilferdings, Ledebours and Crispiens. If we now cast a general glance over a fully completed historical period, namely, from the Paris Commune to the first Socialist Soviet Republic, we shall find that the attitude of Marxism to anarchism in general stands out most definitely and unmistakably. In the final analysis, Marxism proved to be correct, and although the anarchists rightly pointed to the opportunist views on the state that prevailed among the majority of the socialist parties, it must be stated, firstly, that this opportunism was connected with the distortion, and even deliberate suppression, of Marx's views on the state (in my book, *The State and Revolution,* I pointed out that for thirty-six years, from 1875 to 1911, Bebel kept secret a letter by Engels which very vividly, sharply, bluntly and clearly exposed the opportunism of the stock Social-Democratic conceptions of the state); and, secondly, that the rectification of these opportunist views, the recognition of Soviet power and its superiority over bourgeois parliamentary democracy, proceeded most rapidly and extensively precisely among the most Marxian trends in the socialist parties of Europe and America.

On two occasions the struggle that Bolshevism waged against "Left" deviations within its own party assumed particularly large proportions: in 1908, on the question of whether or not to participate in a most reactionary "parliament" and in the legal workers' societies, which were being restricted by most reactionary laws; and again in 1918 (the Brest-Litovsk Peace), on the question whether one or another "compromise" was admissible.

In 1908 the "Left" Bolsheviks were expelled from our Party for stubbornly refusing to understand the necessity of participating in a most reactionary "parliament." The "Lefts" — among whom there were many splendid revolutionaries who subsequently bore (and still bear) the title of member of the Communist Party with credit — based themselves particularly on the successful experience of the boycott in 1905. When, in August 1905, the tsar announced the convocation of an advisory "parliament," the Bolsheviks — in the teeth of all the opposition parties and the Mensheviks — called for a boycott, and it was actually swept away by the revolution of October 1905. At that time the boycott proved correct, not because non-participation in reactionary parliaments is correct in general, but because we correctly gauged the objective situation which was leading to the rapid transformation of the mass strikes into a political strike, then into a revolutionary strike, and then into uprising. Moreover, the struggle at that time centred around the question whether to leave the convocation of the first representative assembly to the tsar, or to attempt to wrest its convocation from the hands of the old regime. When there was no certainty, nor could there be, that the objective situation was analogous, and likewise no certainty of a similar trend and rate of development, the boycott ceased to be correct.

The Bolshevik boycott of "parliament" in 1905 enriched the revolutionary proletariat with highly valuable political experience and showed that in combining legal with illegal, parliamentary with extra-parliamentary forms of struggle, it is sometimes useful and even essential to reject parliamentary forms. But it is a very great mistake indeed to apply this experience blindly, imitatively and uncritically to *other* conditions and to *other* situations. The boycott of the "Duma" by the Bolsheviks in 1906 was, however, a mistake, although a small and easily remediable one.* A boycott of the Duma in 1907, 1908 and subsequent years would have been a serious mistake and one difficult to remedy, because, on the one hand, a very rapid rise of the revolutionary tide and its conversion into an uprising could not be expected, and, on the other hand, the whole historical situation attending the renovation of the bourgeois monarchy called for combining legal and illegal activities. Today, when we turn back at this completed historical period, the connection of which with

---

* What applies to individuals applies — with necessary modifications — to politics and parties. Not he is wise who makes no mistakes. There are no such men nor can there be. He is wise who makes not very serious mistakes and who knows how to correct them easily and quickly.

subsequent periods is fully revealed, it becomes particularly clear that the Bolsheviks *could not have* in 1908-14 preserved (let alone strengthened, developed and reinforced) the firm core of the revolutionary party of the proletariat had they not upheld in strenuous struggle the viewpoint that it is *obligatory* to combine legal and illegal forms of struggle, that it is *obligatory* to participate even in a most reactionary parliament and in a number of other institutions restricted by reactionary laws (sick benefit societies, etc.).

In 1918 things did not reach a split. The "Left" Communists at that time only formed a separate group or "faction" within our Party, and that not for long. In the same year, 1918, the most prominent representatives of "Left Communism," for example, Comrades Radek and Bukharin, openly admitted their mistake. It had seemed to them that the Brest-Litovsk Peace was a compromise with the imperialists that was inadmissible on principle and harmful to the party of the revolutionary proletariat. It was indeed a compromise with the imperialists, but it was a compromise which, under the circumstances, was *obligatory*.

Today, when I hear our tactics during the conclusion of the Brest-Litovsk Peace assailed by the "Socialist-Revolutionaries," for instance, or when I hear the remark made by Comrade Lansbury in conversation with me — "Our British trade union leaders say that if it was permissible for the Bolsheviks to compromise, it is permissible for them to compromise too," I usually reply by first of all giving a simple and "popular" example:

Imagine that your automobile is held up by armed bandits. You hand them over your money, passport, revolver and automobile. In return you are relieved of the pleasant company of the bandits. That is unquestionably a compromise.

22

"Do ut des" ("I give" you money, firearms, automobile, "so that you give" me the opportunity to depart in peace). But it would be difficult to find a sane man who would declare such a compromise to be "inadmissible on principle," or who would proclaim the compromiser an accomplice of the bandits (even though the bandits might use the automobile and the firearms for further robberies). Our compromise with the bandits of German imperialism was a compromise of such a kind.

But when the Mensheviks and Socialist-Revolutionaries in Russia, the Scheidemannites (and to a large extent the Kautskyites) in Germany, Otto Bauer and Friedrich Adler (not to speak of Messrs. Renner and Co.) in Austria, the Renaudels and Longuet and Co. in France, the Fabians, the "Independents" and the "Labourites"[9] in England, in 1914-18 and in 1918-20 entered into *compromises* with the bandits of their own, and sometimes of the "Allied," bourgeoisie *against* the revolutionary proletariat of their own country, all these gentlemen did act as *accomplices in banditry.*

The conclusion is clear: to reject compromises "on principle," to reject the admissibility of compromises in general, no matter of what kind, is childishness, which it is difficult even to take seriously. A political leader who desires to be useful to the revolutionary proletariat must know how to single out *concrete* cases when such compromises are inadmissible, when they are an expression of opportunism and *treachery,* and direct all the force of criticism, the full edge of merciless exposure and relentless war, against *those concrete* compromises, and not allow the past masters at "practical" Socialism and the parliamentary Jesuits to dodge and wriggle out of responsibility by disquisitions on "compromises in general." It is precisely in this way that Messrs. the "leaders" of the British trade unions, as well as the Fabian society and the "Independent" Labour Party, dodge responsibility *for the treachery they have perpetrated*, for having made *such* a compromise that is really tantamount to the worst kind of opportunism, treachery and betrayal.

There are compromises and compromises. One must be able to analyze the situation and the concrete conditions of each compromise, or of each variety of compromise. One must learn to distinguish between a man who gave the bandits money and firearms in order to lessen the damage they can do and facilitate their capture and execution, and a man who gives bandits money and firearms in order to share in the loot. In politics this is by no means always as easy as in this childishly simple example. But anyone who set out to invent a recipe for the workers that would provide in advance ready-made solutions for all cases in life, or who promised that the policy of the revolutionary proletariat would never encounter difficult or intricate situations, would simply be a charlatan.

So as to leave no room for misinterpretation, I shall attempt to outline, if only very briefly, a few fundamental rules for analyzing concrete compromises.

The party which concluded a compromise with the German imperialists by signing the Brest-Litovsk Peace had been working out its internationalism in action ever since the end of 1914. It was not afraid to call for the defeat of the tsarist monarchy and to condemn "defence of the fatherland" in a war between two imperialist robbers. The parliamentary representatives of this party took the road to Siberia rather than the road leading to ministerial portfolios in a bourgeois government. The revolution that overthrew tsardom and established a democratic republic put this party to a new and tremendous test: the party entered into no agreements with its "own" imperialists, but prepared and carried out their overthrow. Having taken over political power, this party did not leave a vestige either of landlord or capitalist property. Having made public and repudiated the secret treaties of the imperialists, this party proposed peace to *all* nations, and yielded to the violence of the Brest-Litovsk robbers only after the Anglo-French imperialists had frustrated the conclusion of a peace, and after the Bolsheviks had done everything humanly possible to hasten the revolution in Germany and other countries. That such a compromise, entered into by such a party in such a situation, was absolutely correct, becomes clearer and more evident to everyone every day.

The Mensheviks and Socialist-Revolutionaries in Russia (like all the leaders of the Second International all over the world in 1914-20) began with treachery by directly or indirectly justifying the "defence of the fatherland," that is, the defence of *their own* predatory bourgeoisie. They continued their treachery by entering into a coalition with the bourgeoisie of *their own* country and fighting together with *their own* bourgeoisie against the revolutionary proletariat of their own country. Their bloc, first with Kerensky[10] and the Cadets,[11] and then with Kolchak and Denikin in Russia, like the bloc of their *confreres* abroad with the bourgeoisie of *their* respective countries, was a desertion to the side of the bourgeoisie against the proletariat. From beginning to end, *their* compromise with the bandits of imperialism lay in the fact that they made themselves *accomplices* in imperialist banditry.

V

"LEFT-WING" COMMUNISM IN GERMANY:
LEADERS — PARTY — CLASS — MASSES

The German Communists of whom we must now speak do not call themselves "Lefts" but, if I am not mistaken, the "opposition on principle." But that they reveal all the symptoms of the "infantile disorder of Leftism" will be seen from what follows.

A pamphlet written from the standpoint of this opposition, and entitled *The Split in the Communist Party of Germany* (*The Spartacus League*), published by "the local group in Frankfurt am Main," sets forth the substance of the views of this opposition most saliently, precisely, clearly and briefly. A few quotations will suffice to acquaint the reader with the substance of their views:

"The Communist Party is the party of the most determined class struggle. . . ."

". . . Politically, the transition period (between capitalism and Socialism) is the period of the proletarian dictatorship. . . ."

"The question arises: Who should be the vehicle of this dictatorship: *the Communist Party or the proletarian class*? . . . Should we on *principle* strive for the dictatorship of the Communist Party, or for the dictatorship of the proletarian class?" . . .

(All italics in the original.)

Further, the author of the pamphlet accuses the "C.C." of the Communist Party of Germany of seeking to reach a *coalition with the Independent Social-Democratic Party of Germany*, of raising "*the question of recognizing in principle all political means*" of struggle, including parliamentarism, only in order to conceal its real and main efforts to form a coalition with the Independents. And the pamphlet goes on to say:

"The opposition has chosen another road. It is of the opinion that the question of the rule of the Communist Party and of the dictatorship of the Party is only a question of tactics. In any case, the rule of the Communist Party is the final form of all party rule. *On principle*, we must strive for the dictatorship of the proletarian class. And all the measures of the Party, its organization, its methods of struggle, its strategy and tactics should be directed to this end. Accordingly, one must emphatically reject all compromise with other parties, all reversion to parliamentary forms of struggle, which have become historically and politically obsolete, all policy of manoeuvring and agreement. . . . Specifically proletarian methods of revolutionary struggle must be strongly emphasized. New forms of organization must be created upon the widest basis and with the widest scope in order to enlist the broadest proletarian circles and strata, which are to take part in the revolutionary struggle under the leadership of the Communist Party. The rallying point for all revolutionary elements should be the *Workers' Union*, based on factory organizations. It should embrace all the workers who follow the slogan: 'Leave the trade unions!' and will organize the fighting proletariat in the broadest battle ranks. Recognition of the class struggle, the Soviet system and the dictatorship should be sufficient for admittance. All subsequent political training of the fighting masses and their political orientation in the struggle is the task of the Communist Party, which stands outside the Workers' Union. . . .

"Consequently, two Communist Parties are now arrayed one against the other:

"*One is a party of leaders*, which strives to organize the revolutionary struggle and to direct it from *above*, resorting to compromises and parliamentarism in order to create a situation which would enable it to enter a coalition government in whose hands the dictatorship would rest.

"The other is a mass party, which expects an upsurge of the revolutionary struggle from *below*, knowing and applying only one method in the struggle, a method which clearly leads to the goal, and rejecting all parliamentary and opportunist methods; this one method is the unconditional *overthrow of the bourgeoisie* with the object of then establishing the proletarian class dictatorship for the accomplishment of Socialism. . . .

". . . There, the dictatorship of leaders; here, the dictatorship of the masses! That is our slogan."

Such are the most essential points characterizing the views of the opposition in the German Communist Party.

Any Bolshevik who has consciously participated in, or has closely observed, the development of Bolshevism since 1903 will at once say after reading these arguments, "What old and familiar rubbish! What 'Left' childishness!"

But let us examine these arguments a little more closely.

The mere presentation of the question — "dictatorship of the Party *or* dictatorship of the class, dictatorship (Party) of the leaders, *or* dictatorship (Party) of the masses?" — testifies to the most incredible and hopeless confusion of mind. These people are straining to *invent* something quite out of the ordinary, and, in their effort to be clever, make themselves ridiculous. Everyone knows that the masses are divided into classes; that the masses can be contrasted to classes only by contrasting the vast majority in general, regardless of division according to status in the social system of production, to categories holding a definite status in the social system of production; that usually, and in the majority of cases, at least in modern civilized countries, classes are led by political parties; that political parties, as a general rule, are directed by more or less stable groups composed of the most authoritative, influential and experienced members, who are elected to the most responsible positions and are called leaders. All this is elementary. All this is simple and clear. Why replace this by some rigmarole, by some new Volapük?[12] On the one hand, these people apparently got confused when they found themselves in difficult straits, when the Party's abrupt change-over from legality to illegality disturbed the customary, normal and simple relations between leaders, parties and classes. In Germany, as in other European countries, people had become too accustomed to legality, to the free and proper election of "leaders" at regular party congresses, to the convenient method of testing the class composition of parties through parliamentary elections, mass meetings, the press, the sentiments of the trade unions and other organizations, etc. When, instead of this customary procedure, it became necessary, due to the stormy development of the revolution and the development of the civil war, to pass quickly from legality to illegality, to combine the two, and to adopt the "inconvenient" and "undemocratic" methods of singling out, or forming, or preserving "groups of leaders" — people lost their heads and began to think up some supernatural nonsense. Probably, the Dutch Tribunists[13] who had the misfortune to be born in a small country where traditions and conditions of legality were particularly privileged and particularly stable, and who had never witnessed the change-over from legality to illegality, became confused, lost their heads, and helped to create these absurd inventions.

On the other hand, we see a simply thoughtless and incoherent use of the now "fashionable" terms "masses" and "leaders." These people have heard and committed to memory a great many attacks on "leaders," in which they are contrasted to "the masses"; but they were unable to think matters out and gain a clear understanding of what it was all about.

The divergence between "leaders" and "masses" was brought out with particular clarity and sharpness in all countries at the end of and after the imperialist war. The principal reason for this phenomenon was explained many times by Marx and Engels between the years 1852 and 1892 by the example of England. That country's monopoly position led to the separation from the "masses" of a semi-petty-bourgeois, opportunist "labour aristocracy." The leaders of this labour aristocracy constantly deserted to the bourgeoisie, and were directly or indirectly in its pay. Marx earned the honour of incurring the hatred of these scoundrels by openly branding them as traitors. Modern (twentieth century) imperialism created a privileged, monopoly position for a few advanced countries, and this gave rise everywhere in the Second International to a certain type of traitor, opportunist, social-chauvinist leaders, who champion the interests of their own craft, their own section of the labour aristocracy. This divorced the opportunist parties from the "masses," that is, from the broadest strata of the working people, from their majority, from the lowest-paid workers. The victory of the revolutionary proletariat is impossible unless this evil is combated, unless the opportunist, social-traitor leaders are exposed, discredited and expelled. And that is the policy on which the Third International embarked.

To go so far in this connection as to contrast, *in general*, dictatorship of the masses to dictatorship of the leaders is ridiculously absurd and stupid. What is particularly curious is that actually, in place of the old leaders, who hold the common human views on ordinary matters, *new leaders* are put forth (under cover of the slogan: "Down with the leaders!") who talk unnatural stuff and nonsense. Such are Lauffenberg, Wolfheim, Horner,[14] Karl Schröder, Friedrich Wendel and Karl Erler* in Germany. Erler's attempts to render the question "more profound" and to proclaim that political parties are generally unnecessary and "bourgeois," represent such Herculean pillars of absurdity that one can only shrug one's shoulders. It goes to confirm the truth that a little mistake can always be turned into a monstrous one if it is persisted in, if profound justifications are sought for it, and if it is carried to its "logical conclusion."

Repudiation of the party principle and of party discipline — such is the opposition's *net result*. And this is tantamount to completely disarming the proletariat *in the interest of the bourgeoisie*. It is tantamount to that petty-bourgeois diffuseness, instability, incapacity for sustained effort, unity and organized action, which, if indulged in, must inevitably destroy every proletarian revolutionary movement. From the standpoint of Communism, the repudiation of the party principle means trying to leap from the eve of the collapse of capitalism (in Germany), not to the lower, or the intermediate,

---

* Karl Erler, "The Dissolution of the Party," *Kommunistische Arbeiterzeitung*,[15] Hamburg, February 7, 1920, No. 32: "The working class cannot destroy the bourgeois state without destroying bourgeois democracy, and it cannot destroy bourgeois democracy without destroying parties."

The more muddleheaded of the syndicalists and anarchists of the Latin countries may derive "satisfaction" from the fact that solid Germans, who evidently consider themselves Marxists (K. Erler and K. Horner show very solidly by their articles in the above-mentioned paper that they consider themselves solid Marxists, but talk incredible nonsense in a most ridiculous manner and reveal their failure to understand the ABC of Marxism), go to the length of making utterly inept statements. The mere acceptance of Marxism does not save one from mistakes. We Russians know this particularly well, because in our country Marxism has been very often the "fashion."

but to the higher phase of Communism. We in Russia (in the third year since the overthrow of the bourgeoisie) are going through the first steps in the transition from capitalism to Socialism, or the lower stage of Communism. Classes have remained, and will remain everywhere *for years after* the conquest of power by the proletariat. Perhaps in England, where there is no peasantry (but where there are small owners!), this period may be shorter. The abolition of classes — means not only driving out the landlords and capitalists — that we accomplished with comparative ease — it also means *abolishing the small commodity producers,* and they *c a n n o t b e   d r i v e n   o u t,* or crushed; we *must live in harmony* with them; they can (and must) be remoulded and re-educated only by very prolonged, slow, cautious organizational work. They encircle the proletariat on every side with a petty-bourgeois atmosphere, which permeates and corrupts the proletariat and causes constant relapses among the proletariat into petty-bourgeois spinelessness, disunity, individualism, and alternate moods of exaltation and dejection. The strictest centralization and discipline are required within the political party of the proletariat in order to counteract this, in order that the *organizational* role of the proletariat (and that is its *principal* role) may be exercised correctly, successfully, victoriously. The dictatorship of the proletariat is a persistent struggle — bloody and bloodless, violent and peaceful, military and economic, educational and administrative — against the forces and traditions of the old society. The force of habit of millions and tens of millions is a most terrible force. Without an iron party tempered in the struggle, without a party enjoying the confidence of all that is honest in the given class, without a party capable of watching and influencing the mood of the masses, it is impossible to conduct such a struggle successfully. It is a thousand times easier to vanquish the centralized big bourgeoisie than to "vanquish" the millions and millions of small owners; yet they, by their ordinary, everyday, imperceptible, elusive, demoralizing activity, achieve the *very* results which the bourgeoisie need and which tend to *restore* the bourgeoisie. Whoever weakens ever so little the iron discipline of the party of the proletariat (especially during the time of *its* dictatorship), actually aids the bourgeoisie against the proletariat.

Side by side with the question of leaders — party — class — masses, we must discuss the question of the "reactionary" trade unions. But first I shall take the liberty of making a few concluding remarks based on the experience of our Party. There *have always been* attacks on the "dictatorship of leaders" in our Party. The first time I heard such attacks, I recall, was in 1895, when, officially, no party yet existed, but when a central group began to be formed in St. Petersburg which was to undertake the leadership of the district groups. At the Ninth Congress of our Party (April 1920) there was a small opposition which also spoke against the "dictatorship of leaders," against the "oligarchy," and so on. There is therefore nothing surprising, nothing new, nothing terrible in the "infantile disorder" of "Left-wing Communism" among the Germans. The illness does not involve any danger, and after it the constitution becomes even stronger. On the other hand, in our case, the rapid alternation of legal and illegal work, which made it particularly necessary to "conceal," to cloak in particular secrecy precisely the general staff, precisely the leaders, sometimes gave rise to extremely dangerous phenomena. The worst was that in 1912 the agent-provocateur Malinovsky got on the

Bolshevik Central Committee. He betrayed scores and scores of the best and most loyal comrades, caused them to be sent to penal servitude and hastened the death of many of them. That he did not cause still greater harm was due to the fact that we had a proper relationship between legal and illegal work. As a member of the Central Committee of the Party and a deputy to the Duma, Malinovsky was forced, in order to gain our confidence, to aid us in establishing legal daily papers, which even under tsardom were able to wage a struggle against the opportunism of the Mensheviks and to propagate the fundamentals of Bolshevism in a suitably disguised form. While Malinovsky with one hand sent scores and scores of the best Bolsheviks to penal servitude and to death, he was obliged with the other to assist in the education of scores and scores of thousands of new Bolsheviks through the medium of the legal press. Those German (as well as British, American, French and Italian) comrades who are confronted with the task of learning how to conduct revolutionary work inside the reactionary trade unions, would do well to give serious thought to this fact.*

In many countries, including the most advanced, the bourgeoisie is undoubtedly now sending agents-provocateurs

---

* Malinovsky was a prisoner-of-war in Germany. When he returned to Russia under the rule of the Bolsheviks, he was instantly put on trial and shot by our workers. The Mensheviks attacked us most bitterly for our mistake — the fact that an agent-provocateur had become a member of the Central Committee of our Party. But when, under Kerensky, we demanded the arrest and trial of Rodzyanko, the Speaker of the Duma, because he had known even before the war that Malinovsky was an agent-provocateur and *had not informed* the Trudoviki[16] and the workers in the Duma, neither the Mensheviks nor the Socialist-Revolutionaries in the Kerensky government supported our demand, and Rodzyanko remained at large and went off unhindered to join Denikin.

into the Communist parties and will continue to do so. One method of combating this peril is by skilfully combining illegal and legal work.

VI

SHOULD REVOLUTIONARIES WORK
IN REACTIONARY TRADE UNIONS?

The German "Lefts" consider that as far as they are
concerned the reply to this question is an unqualified negative.
In their opinion, declamations and angry ejaculations (such
as uttered by K. Horner in a particularly "solid" and particularly stupid manner) against "reactionary" and "counter-
revolutionary" trade unions are sufficient "proof" that it is
unnecessary and even impermissible for revolutionaries and
Communists to work in yellow, social-chauvinist, compromising, counter-revolutionary trade unions of the Legien type.

But however strongly the German "Lefts" may be convinced of the revolutionism of such tactics, these tactics are
in fact fundamentally wrong, and amount to no more than
empty phrase-mongering.

To make this clear, I shall begin with our own experience —
in keeping with the general plan of the present pamphlet,
the object of which is to apply to Western Europe whatever
is of general application, general validity and generally
binding force in the history and the present tactics of
Bolshevism.

The correlation between leaders — Party — class — masses, as well as the relation of the dictatorship of the proletariat and its party to the trade unions, now present themselves concretely in Russia in the following form: the dictatorship is exercised by the proletariat, organized in the Soviets; the proletariat is led by the Communist Party (Bolsheviks), which, according to the data of the last Party Congress (April 1920), has a membership of 611,000. The membership fluctuated greatly both before and after the October Revolution, and was formerly considerably less, even in 1918 and 1919.[17] We are afraid of an excessive growth of the Party, because careerists and charlatans, who deserve only to be shot, inevitably strive to attach themselves to the ruling party. The last time we opened wide the doors of the Party — for workers and peasants only — was during the days (the winter of 1919) when Yudenich was within a few versts of Petrograd, and Denikin was in Orel (about 350 versts from Moscow), that is, when the Soviet Republic was in desperate, mortal danger, and when adventurers, careerists, charlatans and unreliable persons generally could not possibly count on making a profitable career (and had more reason to expect the gallows and torture) by joining the Communists. The Party, which holds annual congresses (the last on the basis of one delegate for each 1,000 members), is directed by a Central Committee of nineteen elected at the congress, and the current work in Moscow has to be carried on by still smaller bodies, viz., the so-called "Orgburo" (Organization Bureau) and "Politburo" (Political Bureau), which are elected at plenary meetings of the Central Committee, five members of the Central Committee to each bureau. This, it would appear, is a full-fledged "oligarchy." Not a single important political or organizational question is decided by

37

any state institution in our republic without the guiding instructions of the Central Committee of the Party.

In its work, the Party relies directly on the *trade unions,* which, at present, according to the data of the last congress (April 1920), have over 4,000,000 members, and which are formally *non-party.* Actually, all the directing bodies of the vast majority of the unions, and primarily, of course, of the all-Russian general trade union centre or bureau (the All-Russian Central Council of Trade Unions), consist of Communists and carry out all the directives of the Party. Thus, on the whole, we have a formally non-Communist, flexible and relatively wide and very powerful proletarian apparatus, by means of which the Party is closely linked up with the *class* and with the *masses,* and by means of which, under the leadership of the Party, the *dictatorship of the class* is exercised. Without close contact with the trade unions, without their hearty support and self-sacrificing work, not only in economic, *but also in military* affairs, it would, of course, have been impossible for us to govern the country and to maintain the dictatorship for two-and-a-half months, let alone two-and-a-half years. Naturally, in practice, this close contact calls for very complicated and diversified work in the form of propaganda, agitation, timely and frequent conferences, not only with the leading trade union workers, but with influential trade union workers generally; it calls for a determined struggle against the Mensheviks, who still have a certain, though very small, number of adherents, whom they teach all possible counter-revolutionary tricks, from ideologically defending democracy (*bourgeois*) and preaching "independence" of the trade unions (independent of the proletarian state power!) to sabotaging proletarian discipline, etc., etc.

We consider that contact with the "masses" through trade unions is not enough. In the course of the revolution practical activities have given rise to *non-party workers' and peasants' conferences,* and we strive by every means to support, develop and extend this institution in order to be able to follow the sentiments of the masses, to come closer to them, to respond to their requirements, to promote the best among them to state posts, etc. Under a recent decree on the transformation of the People's Commissariat of State Control into the "Workers' and Peasants' Inspection," non-party conferences of this kind are given the right to elect members of the State Control for various kinds of investigations, etc.

Then, of course, all the work of the Party is carried on through the Soviets, which embrace the working masses irrespective of occupation. The district congresses of Soviets are *democratic* institutions the like of which even the best of the democratic republics of the bourgeois world has never known; and through these congresses (whose proceedings the Party endeavours to follow with the closest attention), as well as by continually appointing class-conscious workers to various posts in the rural districts, the role of the proletariat as leader of the peasantry is exercised, the dictatorship of the urban proletariat is realized, a systematic struggle against the rich, bourgeois, exploiting and profiteering peasantry is waged, etc.

Such is the general mechanism of the proletarian state power viewed "from above," from the standpoint of the practical realization of the dictatorship. It can be hoped that the reader will understand why the Russian Bolshevik who is acquainted with this mechanism and who for twenty-five years has watched it growing out of small, illegal, underground circles, cannot help regarding all this talk about "from above" *o r* "from below," about the dictatorship of leaders *o r* the dictatorship of the masses, etc., as ridiculous and childish nonsense, something like discussing whether a man's left leg or right arm is more useful to him.

And we cannot but regard as equally ridiculous and childish nonsense the pompous, very learned, and frightfully revolutionary disquisitions of the German Lefts to the effect that Communists cannot and should not work in reactionary trade unions, that it is permissible to turn down such work, that it is necessary to leave the trade unions and to create an absolutely brand-new, immaculate "Workers' Union" invented by very nice (and, probably, for the most part very youthful) Communists, etc., etc.

Capitalism inevitably leaves Socialism the legacy, on the one hand, of old trade and craft distinctions among the workers, distinctions evolved in the course of centuries; and, on the other hand, trade unions which only very slowly, in the course of years and years, can and will develop into broader, industrial unions with less of the craft union about them (embracing whole industries, and not only crafts, trades and occupations), and later proceed, through these industrial unions, to eliminate the division of labour among people, to educate, school and train people with *an all-round development and an all-round* training, people who *know how to do everything.* Communism is advancing and must advance towards this goal, and *will reach it,* but only after very many years. To attempt in practice today to anticipate this future result of a fully developed, fully stabilized and formed, fully expanded and mature Communism would be like trying to teach higher mathematics to a four-year-old child.

We can (and must) begin to build Socialism, not with imaginary human material, nor with human material specially prepared by us, but with the human material bequeathed to us by capitalism. True, that is very "difficult," but no other approach to this task is serious enough to warrant discussion.

The trade unions were a tremendous progressive step for the working class in the early days of capitalist development, inasmuch as they represented a transition from the disunity and helplessness of the workers to the *rudiments* of class organization. When the *highest* form of proletarian class organization began to arise, viz., the *revolutionary party of the proletariat* (which will not deserve the name until it learns to bind the leaders with the class and the masses into one single indissoluble whole), the trade unions inevitably began to reveal *certain* reactionary features, a certain craft narrowness, a certain tendency to be nonpolitical, a certain inertness, etc. But the development of the proletariat did not, and could not, proceed anywhere in the world otherwise than through the trade unions, through reciprocal action between them and the party of the working class. The conquest of political power by the proletariat is a gigantic forward step for the proletariat as a class, and the Party must more than ever and in a new way, not only in the old way, educate and guide the trade unions, at the same time bearing in mind that they are and will long remain an indispensable "school of Communism" and a preparatory school that trains the proletarians to exercise their dictatorship, an indispensable organization of the workers for the gradual transfer of the management of the whole economic life of the country to the working *class* (and not to the separate trades), and later to all the working people.

A *certain* amount of "reactionariness" in the trade unions, in the sense mentioned, is *inevitable* under the dictatorship of the proletariat. Failure to understand this signifies complete failure to understand the fundamental conditions of the *transition* from capitalism to Socialism. To fear *this* "reactionariness," to try to *avoid* it, to leap over it, would be the greatest folly, for it would be fearing that function of the proletarian vanguard which consists in training, educating, enlightening and drawing into the new life the most backward strata and masses of the working class and the peasantry. On the other hand, to postpone the achievement of the dictatorship of the proletariat until a time comes when not a single worker is left with a narrow craft outlook, or with craft and craft-union prejudices, would be a still greater mistake. The art of politics (and the Communist's correct understanding of his tasks) lies in correctly gauging the conditions and the moment when the vanguard of the proletariat can successfully seize power, when it is able, during and after the seizure of power, to obtain adequate support from adequately broad strata of the working class and of the non-proletarian working masses, and when it is able thereafter to maintain, consolidate and extend its rule by educating, training and attracting ever broader masses of the working people.

Further. In countries more advanced than Russia, a certain reactionariness in the trade unions has been and was bound to be manifested to a much stronger degree than in our country. Our Mensheviks found support in the trade unions (and to some extent still find in a very few unions), precisely because of the craft narrowness, craft egotism and opportunism. The Mensheviks of the West have acquired a much firmer "footing" in the trade unions; there the *craft-union, narrow-minded, selfish, casehardened, covetous, petty-bourgeois "labour aristocracy," imperialist-minded, imperialist-bribed and imperialist-corrupted,* emerged as a much stronger stratum than in our country. That is incontestable. The struggle against the Gomperses, against Messrs. Jouhaux, Henderson, Merrheim, Legien and Co. in Western Europe is much more difficult than the struggle against our Mensheviks, who represent an *absolutely homogeneous* social and political type. This struggle must be waged ruthlessly, and it must unfailingly be brought — as we brought it — to a point when all the incorrigible leaders of opportunism and social-chauvinism are completely discredited and driven out of the trade unions. Political power cannot be captured (and the attempt to capture it should not be made) until the struggle has reached a *certain* stage. This "certain stage" will be *different* in different countries and in different circumstances; it can be correctly gauged only by thoughtful, experienced and knowledgeable political leaders of the proletariat in each particular country. (In Russia, one among other criteria of the success of this struggle was the elections to the Constituent Assembly in November 1917, a few days after the proletarian revolution of October 25, 1917. In these elections the Mensheviks were utterly defeated; they obtained 700,000 votes — 1,400,000 if the vote of Transcaucasia be added — as against 9,000,000 votes polled by the Bolsheviks. See my article, "The Elections to the Constituent Assembly and the Dictatorship of the Proletariat,"[18] in the *Communist International*, No. 7-8.)

But we wage the struggle against the "labour aristocracy" in the name of the masses of the workers and in order to win them to our side; we wage the struggle against the opportunist and social-chauvinist leaders in order to win the working class to our side. To forget this most elementary and most self-evident truth would be stupid. And it is precisely this stupidity the German "Left" Communists are guilty of when, *because* of the reactionary and counter-revolutionary character of the trade union *top leadership,* they jump to the conclusion that . . . we must leave the trade unions!! that we must refuse to work in them!! that we must create new and *a r t i f i c i a l* forms of labour organization!! This is such an unpardonable blunder that it is equal to the greatest service the Communists could render the bourgeoisie. For our Mensheviks, like all the opportunist, social-chauvinist, Kautskyite trade union leaders, are nothing but "agents of the bourgeoisie in the working-class movement" (as we have always said the Mensheviks were), or "labour lieutenants of the capitalist class," to use the splendid and profoundly true expression of the followers of Daniel DeLeon in America. To refuse to work in the reactionary trade unions means leaving the insufficiently developed or backward masses of workers under the influence of the reactionary leaders, the agents of the bourgeoisie, the labour aristocrats, or the "workers who have become completely bourgeois" (cf. Engels' letter to Marx in 1858 about the British workers[19]).

It is precisely this absurd "theory" that Communists must not work in reactionary trade unions that brings out with the greatest clarity how frivolous is the attitude of the "Left" Communists towards the question of influencing "the masses," and to what abuses they go in their vociferations about "the masses." If you want to help "the masses" and to win the sympathy and support of "the masses," you must not fear difficulties, you must not fear the pinpricks, chicanery, insults and persecution on the part of the "leaders" (who, being opportunists and social-chauvinists, are in most cases directly or indirectly connected with the bourgeoisie and the police), but must imperatively *work wherever the masses are to be found.* You must be capable of every sacrifice, of overcoming the greatest obstacles in order to carry on agitation and propaganda systematically, perseveringly, persistently and patiently, precisely in those institutions, societies and associations — even the most ultra-reactionary — in which proletarian or semiproletarian masses are to be found. And the trade unions and workers' cooperatives (the latter sometimes, at least) are precisely organizations where the masses are to be found. According to figures quoted in the Swedish paper *Folkets Dagblad Politiken* on March 10, 1920, trade union membership in Great Britain increased from 5,500,000 at the end of 1917 to 6,600,000 at the end of 1918, an increase of 19 per cent. Towards the close of 1919 the membership was estimated at 7,500,000. I have not at hand the corresponding figures for France and Germany, but absolutely incontestable and generally known facts testify to a rapid growth of trade union membership in these countries too.

These facts make crystal clear what is confirmed by thousands of other symptoms, namely, that class consciousness and the desire for organization are growing precisely among the proletarian masses, among the "rank and file," among the backward elements. Millions of workers in Great Britain, France and Germany are *for the first time* passing from a complete lack of organization to the elementary, lowest, most simple, and (for those still thoroughly imbued with bourgeois-democratic prejudices) most easily comprehensible form of organization, namely, the trade unions; yet the revolutionary, but imprudent, Left Communists stand by, shouting "the masses, the masses!" — and *refuse to work within the t r a d e u n i o n s* !! refuse on the pretext that they are "reactionary"!! and invent a brand-new, immaculate little "Workers' Union," which is guiltless of bourgeois-democratic prejudices and innocent of craft or narrow craft-union sins, which, they claim, will be (will be!) a broad organization, and the only (only!) condition of membership of which will be "recognition of the Soviet system and the dictatorship"!! (See passage quoted above.)

Greater foolishness and greater damage to the revolution than that caused by the "Left" revolutionaries cannot be imagined! Why, if we in Russia today, after two and a half years of unprecedented victories over the bourgeoisie of Russia and the Entente, were to make "recognition of the dictatorship" a condition of trade union membership, we should be committing a folly, we should be damaging our influence over the masses, we should be helping the Mensheviks. For the whole task of the Communists is to be able to *convince* the backward elements, to work *among* them, and not to *fence themselves off* from them by artificial and childishly "Left" slogans.

There need be no doubt that Messrs. Gompers, Henderson, Jouhaux, and Legien are very grateful to "Left" revolutionaries who, like the German opposition "on principle" (heaven preserve us from such "principles"!), or like some of the revolutionaries in the American Industrial Workers of the World,[20] advocate leaving the reactionary trade unions and refusal to work in them. There need be no doubt that those gentlemen, the "leaders" of opportunism, will resort to every trick of bourgeois diplomacy, to the aid of bourgeois governments, the priests, the police and the courts, to prevent Communists joining the trade unions, to force them out by every means, to make their work in the trade unions as unpleasant as possible, to insult, bait and persecute them. We must be able to withstand all this, to agree to all and every sacrifice, and even — if need be — to resort to various stratagems, artifices, illegal methods, to evasions and subterfuges, only so as to get into the trade unions, to remain in them, and to carry on Communist work within them at all costs. Under tsardom we had no "legal possibilities" whatever until 1905; but when Zubatov, a secret police agent, organized Black-Hundred workers' assemblies and workingmen's societies for the purpose of trapping revolutionaries and combating them, we sent members of our Party to these assemblies and into these societies (I personally remember one of them, Comrade Babushkin, a prominent St. Petersburg worker, who was shot by the tsar's generals in 1906). They established contact with the masses, managed to carry on their agitation, and succeeded in wresting workers from the influence of Zubatov's agents.* Of course, in Western Europe, where legalistic, constitutionalist, bourgeois-democratic prejudices have a particular tenacity and are very deeply ingrained, this is a more difficult job. But it can and should be carried out, and carried out systematically.

The Executive Committee of the Third International must, in my opinion, positively condemn, and call upon the next congress of the Communist International to condemn, both the policy of refusing to join reactionary trade unions in general (explaining in detail why such refusal is unwise, and what extreme harm it does to the cause of the proletarian revolution) and, in particular, the line of conduct of some members of the Communist Party of Holland, who — whether directly or indirectly, openly or covertly, wholly or partly does not matter — supported this erroneous policy. The Third Inter-

---

* The Gomperses, Hendersons, Jouhaux and Legiens are nothing but Zubatovs, differing from our Zubatov only in their European dress, polish, civilized, refined, democratically sleek manner of conducting their despicable policy.

national must break with the tactics of the Second International; it must not evade or gloss over sore points, but must put them bluntly. The whole truth has been put squarely to the "Independents" (the Independent Social-Democratic Party of Germany); the whole truth must likewise be put squarely to the "Left" Communists.

VII

SHOULD WE PARTICIPATE
IN BOURGEOIS PARLIAMENTS?

The German "Left" Communists, with the greatest contempt — and with the greatest frivolity — reply to this question in the negative. Their arguments? In the passage quoted above we read:

"... One must emphatically reject ... all reversion to parliamentary forms of struggle, which have become historically and politically obsolete. ..."

This is said with absurd pretentiousness, and is obviously incorrect. "Reversion" to parliamentarism! Perhaps there is already a Soviet republic in Germany? It seems not! How, then, can one speak of "reversion"? Is this not an empty phrase?

Parliamentarism has become "historically obsolete." That is true as regards propaganda. But everyone knows that this is still a long way from overcoming it *practically*. Capitalism could have been declared, and with full justice, to be "historically obsolete" many decades ago, but that does not at all remove the need for a very long and very persistent struggle *on the soil* of capitalism. Parliamentarism is "historically obsolete" from the standpoint of *world history,* that is to say, the *era* of bourgeois parliamentarism has come to an end and the *era* of the proletarian dictatorship has *begun.* That is incontestable. But world history reckons in decades. Ten or twenty years sooner or later makes no difference when measured by the scale of world history; from the standpoint of world history it is a trifle that cannot be calculated even approximately. But precisely for that reason it is a howling theoretical blunder to apply the scale of world history to practical politics.

Is parliamentarism "politically obsolete"? That is quite another matter. Were that true, the position of the "Lefts" would be a strong one. But it has to be proved by a most searching analysis, and the "Lefts" do not even know how to approach it. In the "Theses on Parliamentarism," published in the *Bulletin of the Provisional Bureau in Amsterdam of the Communist International,* No. 1, February 1920, and obviously expressing the Dutch-Left or Left-Dutch strivings, the analysis, as we shall see, is also hopelessly bad.

In the first place, contrary to the opinion of such outstanding political leaders as Rosa Luxemburg and Karl Liebknecht, the German "Lefts," as we know, considered parliamentarism to be "politically obsolete" even in January 1919. We know that the "Lefts" were mistaken. This fact alone utterly destroys, at a single stroke, the proposition that parliamentarism is "politically obsolete." The obligation falls upon the "Lefts" of proving why their error, indisputable at that time, has now ceased to be an error. They do not, and cannot, produce even a shadow of proof. The attitude of a political party towards its own mistakes is one of the most important and surest ways of judging how earnest the party is and how it *in practice* fulfils its obligations towards its *class* and the toiling *masses*. Frankly admitting a mistake, ascertaining the reasons for it, analyzing the conditions which led to it, and thoroughly discussing the means of correcting it — that is the earmark of a serious party; that is the way it should perform its duties, that is the way it should educate and train the *class,* and then the *masses*. By failing to fulfil this duty, by failing to give the utmost attention, care and consideration to the study of their obvious mistake, the "Lefts" in Germany (and in Holland), have proved that they are not a *party of the class,* but a circle, not a *party of the masses,* but a group of intellectuals and of a few workers who imitate the worst features of intellectualism.

Secondly, in the same pamphlet of the Frankfurt group of "Lefts" that we have already cited in detail, we read:

". . . The millions of workers who still follow the policy of the Centre" (the Catholic "Centre" Party) "are counter-revolutionary. The rural proletarians provide the legions of counter-revolutionary troops." (Page 3 of the pamphlet.)

Everything goes to show that this statement is much too sweeping and exaggerated. But the basic fact set forth here is incontrovertible, and its acknowledgement by the "Lefts" is particularly clear evidence of their mistake. How can one say that "parliamentarism is politically obsolete," when "millions" and "legions" of *proletarians* are not only still in favour of parliamentarism in general, but are downright "counter-revolutionary"!? Clearly, parliamentarism in Germany is *not yet* politically obsolete. Clearly, the "Lefts" in Germany have mistaken *their desire,* their political-ideological attitude, for objective reality. That is the most dangerous mistake for revolutionaries. In Russia — where, over a particularly long period and in particularly varied forms, the extremely fierce and savage yoke of tsardom produced revolutionaries of diverse shades, revolutionaries who displayed astonishing devotion, enthusiasm, heroism and strength of will — in Russia we have observed this mistake of the revolutionaries very closely, we have studied it very attentively and have first-hand knowledge of it; and we can therefore notice it especially clearly in others. Parliamentarism, of course, is "politically obsolete" for the Communists in Germany; but — and that is the whole point — we must *not* regard what is obsolete *for us* as being obsolete *for the class,* as being obsolete *for the masses.* Here again we find that the "Lefts" do not know how to reason, do not know how to act as the party of the *class,* as the party of the *masses.* You must not sink to the level of the masses, to the level of the backward strata of the class. That is incontestable. You must tell them the bitter truth. You must call their bourgeois-democratic and parliamentary prejudices — prejudices. But at the same time you must *soberly* follow the *actual* state of class consciousness and preparedness of the whole class (not only of its Communist vanguard), of all the toiling *masses* (not only of their advanced elements).

Even if not "millions" and "legions," but only a fairly large *minority* of industrial workers follow the Catholic priests — and a similar minority of rural workers follow the landlords and kulaks (Grossbauern) — it *undoubtedly* follows that parliamentarism in Germany is *not yet* politically obsolete, that participation in parliamentary elections and in the struggle on the parliamentary rostrum is *obligatory* for the party of the revolutionary proletariat *precisely* for the purpose of educating the backward strata of *its own class,* precisely for the purpose of awakening and enlightening the undeveloped, downtrodden, ignorant rural *masses.* As long as you are unable to disperse the bourgeois parliament and every other type of reactionary institution, you *must* work inside them *precisely* because there you will still find workers who are doped by the priests and by the dreariness of rural life; otherwise you risk becoming mere babblers.

Thirdly, the "Left" Communists have a great deal to say in praise of us Bolsheviks. One sometimes feels like telling them to praise us less and try to understand the tactics of the Bolsheviks more, to familiarize themselves with them more! We took part in the elections to the Russian bourgeois parliament, the Constituent Assembly, in September-November 1917. Were our tactics correct or not? If not, then this should be clearly stated and proved, for it is essential in working out correct tactics for international Communism. If they were correct, then we must draw certain conclusions. Of course, there can be no question of regarding conditions in Russia on a par with conditions in Western Europe. But as regards the special question of the meaning of the concept that "parliamentarism has become politically obsolete," it is essential to take careful account of our experience, for unless concrete experience is taken into account such concepts very easily turn into empty phrases. Did not we, the Russian Bolsheviks, have more right in September-November 1917 than any Western Communists to consider that parliamentarism was politically obsolete in Russia? Of course we did, for the point is not whether bourgeois parliaments have existed for a long time or a short time, but how far the broad masses of the working people are *prepared* (ideologically, politically and practically) to accept the Soviet system and to disperse the bourgeois-democratic parliament (or allow it to be dispersed). That, owing to a number of special conditions, the urban working class and the soldiers and peasants of Russia were in September-November 1917 exceptionally well prepared to accept the Soviet system and to disperse the most democratic of bourgeois parliaments, is an absolutely incontestable and fully established historical fact. Nevertheless, the Bolsheviks did *not* boycott the Constituent Assembly, but took part in the elections both before the proletariat conquered political power and *after*. That these elections yielded exceedingly valuable (and for the proletariat, highly useful) political results I have proved, I make bold to hope, in the above-mentioned article, which analyzes in detail the figures of the elections to the Constituent Assembly in Russia.

The conclusion which follows from this is absolutely incontrovertible; it has been proved that participation in a bourgeois-democratic parliament even a few weeks before the victory of a Soviet republic, and even *after* such a victory, not only does not harm the revolutionary proletariat, but actually helps it to *prove* to the backward masses why such parliaments deserve to be dispersed; it *helps* their successful dispersal, and *helps* to make bourgeois parliamentarism "politically obsolete." To refuse to heed this experience, and at the same time to claim affiliation to the Communist *International*, which must work out its tactics *internationally* (not as narrow or one-sided national tactics, but as international tactics), is to commit the gravest blunder and actually to retreat from internationalism while recognizing it in words.

Now let us examine the "Dutch-Left" arguments in favour of nonparticipation in parliaments. The following is the text of the most important of the above-mentioned "Dutch" theses, Thesis No. 4:

"When the capitalistic system of production has broken down, and society is in a state of revolution, parliamentary activity gradually loses importance as compared with the action of the masses themselves. When, then, parliament becomes the centre and organ of the counter-revolution, whilst on the other hand, the labouring class builds up the instruments of its power in the Soviets, it may even prove necessary to abstain from all and any participation in parliamentary action."

The first sentence is obviously wrong, since the action of the masses — a big strike, for instance — is more important than parliamentary activity at *all* times, and not only during a revolution or in a revolutionary situation. This obviously untenable and historically and politically incorrect argument only very clearly shows that the authors absolutely ignore both the general European experience (the French experience before the revolutions of 1848 and 1870; the German experience of 1878-90, etc.) and the Russian experience (see above) as to the importance of *combining* legal with illegal struggle. This question is of immense importance in general, and in particular, because in *all* civilized and advanced countries the time is rapidly approaching when such a combination will more and more become — in part it has already become — obligatory for the party of the revolutionary proletariat owing to the fact that civil war between the proletariat and the bourgeoisie is maturing and approaching, owing to the fierce persecution of the Communists by republican governments and bourgeois governments generally, which resort to any violation of legality (witness the example of America alone!), and so on. This very important question the Dutch, and the Lefts in general, have utterly failed to understand.

As for the second sentence, in the first place it is wrong historically. We Bolsheviks participated in the most counter-revolutionary parliaments, and experience has shown that this participation was not only useful but essential for the party

of the revolutionary proletariat precisely after the first bourgeois revolution in Russia (1905) in order to prepare the way
for the second bourgeois revolution (February 1917), and then
for the socialist revolution (October 1917). In the second
place, this sentence is amazingly illogical. If parliament becomes an organ and a "centre" (in reality it never has been
and never can be a "centre," but that by the way) of counter-revolution, while the workers are building up the instruments of their power in the form of Soviets, it follows
that the workers must prepare — ideologically, politically and
technically — for the struggle of the Soviets against parliament, for the dispersal of parliament by the Soviets. But it
does not follow that this dispersal is hindered, or is not facilitated, by the presence of a Soviet opposition *within* the counter-revolutionary parliament. In the course of our victorious
struggle against Denikin and Kolchak, we never found that
the existence of a Soviet, proletarian opposition in their camp
was immaterial to our victories. We know perfectly well
that the dispersal of the Constituent Assembly on January 5,
1918, far from being hindered, was actually facilitated by the
fact that within the counter-revolutionary Constituent Assembly about to be dispersed there was a consistent, Bolshevik, as well as an inconsistent, Left Socialist-Revolutionary,
Soviet opposition. The authors of the theses are utterly confused and have forgotten the experience of many, if not all,
revolutions, which shows how very useful during a revolution is the combination of mass action outside the reactionary
parliament with an opposition sympathetic to (or, better still,
directly supporting) the revolution inside it. The Dutch,
and the "Lefts" in general, argue like doctrinaire revolutionaries who have never taken part in a real revolution, or
who have never deeply pondered over the history of revolu-

tions, or who have naively mistaken the subjective "rejection" of a certain reactionary institution for its actual destruction by the combined action of a number of objective factors.

The surest way of discrediting and damaging a new political (and not only political) idea is to reduce it to absurdity on the plea of defending it. For every truth, if "overdone" (as Dietzgen senior put it), if exaggerated, if carried beyond the limits of its actual applicability, can be reduced to absurdity, and is even bound to become an absurdity under these conditions. That is just the kind of backhanded service the Dutch and German Lefts are rendering the new truth that the Soviet form of government is superior to bourgeois-democratic parliaments. It stands to reason that anyone who subscribed to the old view, or in general maintained that refusal to participate in bourgeois parliaments is impermissible under any circumstances, would be wrong. I cannot attempt to formulate here the conditions under which a boycott is useful, for the object of this pamphlet is far more modest, namely, to study Russian experience in connection with certain topical questions of international communist tactics. Russian experience has given us one successful and correct (1905) and one incorrect (1906) example of the application of the boycott by the Bolsheviks. Analyzing the first case, we see that we succeeded in *preventing the convocation* of a reactionary parliament by a reactionary government in a situation in which extra-parliamentary, revolutionary mass action (strikes in particular) was mounting with exceptional rapidity, when not a single section of the proletariat and of the peasantry could support the reactionary government in any way, when the revolutionary proletariat was acquiring influence over the broad, backward masses through the strike struggle and the agrarian movement. It is quite obvious that *this* experience is not applicable to present-day European conditions. It is likewise quite obvious — and the foregoing arguments bear this out — that the advocacy, even if with reservations, by the Dutch and other "Lefts" of refusal to participate in parliaments is fundamentally wrong and detrimental to the cause of the revolutionary proletariat.

In Western Europe and America parliament has become especially abhorrent to the advanced revolutionary members of the working class. That is incontestable. It is quite comprehensible, for it is difficult to imagine anything more vile, abominable and treacherous than the behaviour of the vast majority of the Socialist and Social-Democratic parliamentary deputies during and after the war. But it would be not only unreasonable, but actually criminal to yield to this mood when deciding *how* this generally recognized evil should be fought. In many countries of Western Europe the revolutionary mood, we might say, is at present a "novelty," or a "rarity," which had been all too long waited for vainly and impatiently; and perhaps that is why the mood is so easily succumbed to. Certainly, without a revolutionary mood among the masses, and without conditions facilitating the growth of this mood, revolutionary tactics would never be converted into action; but we in Russia have become convinced by very long, painful and bloody experience of the truth that revolutionary tactics cannot be built on revolutionary moods alone. Tactics must be based on a sober and strictly objective appraisal of *all* the class forces of the particular state (and of the states that surround it, and of all states the world over) as well as of the experience of revolutionary movements. To show how "revolutionary" one is solely by hurling abuse at parliamentary opportunism, solely by repudiating participation in parliaments, is very easy; but just because it is too easy, it is not the solution for a difficult, a very difficult problem. It is much more difficult to create a really revolutionary parliamentary group in a European parliament than it was in Russia. Of course. But that is only a particular expression of the general truth that it was easy for Russia, in the specific, historically very unique situation of 1917, to *start* the socialist revolution, but it will be more difficult for Russia than for the European countries to *continue* the revolution and bring it to its consummation. I had occasion to point this out already at the beginning of 1918, and our experience of the past two years has entirely confirmed the correctness of this view. Certain specific conditions, viz., 1) the possibility of linking up the Soviet revolution with the ending, as a consequence of this revolution, of the imperialist war, which had exhausted the workers and peasants to an incredible degree; 2) the possibility of taking advantage for a certain time of the mortal conflict between two world-powerful groups of imperialist robbers, who were unable to unite against their Soviet enemy; 3) the possibility of enduring a comparatively lengthy civil war, partly owing to the enormous size of the country and to the poor means of communication; 4) the existence of such a profound bourgeois-democratic revolutionary movement among the peasantry that the party of the proletariat was able to take the revolutionary demands of the peasant party (the Socialist-Revolutionary Party, the majority of the members of which were definitely hostile to Bolshevism) and realize them at once, thanks to the conquest of political power by the proletariat — these specific conditions do not exist in Western Europe at present; and a repetition of such or similar conditions will not come so easily. That, by the way, apart from a number of other causes, is why it will be more difficult for Western Europe to *start* a socialist revolution than it was for us. To attempt to "circumvent" this difficulty by "skipping" the difficult job of utilizing reactionary parliaments for revolutionary purposes is absolutely childish. You want to create a new society, yet you fear the difficulties involved in forming a good parliamentary group, made up of convinced, devoted, heroic Communists, in a reactionary parliament! Is that not childish? If Karl Liebknecht in Germany and Z. Höglund in Sweden were able, even without mass support from below, to set examples in the truly revolutionary utilization of reactionary parliaments, how can one say that a rapidly growing revolutionary, mass party, in the midst of the postwar disillusionment and embitterment of the masses, cannot *hammer out* a communist group in the worst of parliaments?! Precisely because the backward masses of the workers and — to an even greater degree — of the small peasants are in Western Europe much more imbued with bourgeois-democratic and parliamentary prejudices than they were in Russia, precisely because of that, it is *only* from within such institutions as bourgeois parliaments that Communists can (and must) wage a long and persistent struggle, undaunted by any difficulties, to expose, dissipate and overcome these prejudices.

The German "Lefts" complain about bad "leaders" in their party, give way to despair, and go to the absurd length of "repudiating" "leaders." But when conditions are such that it is often necessary to hide "leaders" underground, the *development* of good, reliable, experienced and authoritative "leaders" is a very difficult matter, and these difficulties *cannot* be successfully overcome without combining legal and illegal work, and *without testing the "leaders," among other ways,* in the parliamentary arena *as well.* Criticism — the keenest, most ruthless and uncompromising criticism — must be directed, not against parliamentarism or parliamentary activities, but against those leaders who are unable — and still more against those who are *unwilling* — to utilize parliamentary elections and the parliamentary tribune in a revolutionary, communist manner. Only such criticism — combined, of course, with the expulsion of incapable leaders and their replacement by capable ones — will constitute useful and fruitful revolutionary work that will simultaneously train the "leaders" to be worthy of the working class and of the toiling masses, and train the masses to be able properly to understand the political situation and the often very complicated and intricate tasks that spring from that situation.*

---

* I have had too little opportunity to acquaint myself with "Left-wing" Communism in Italy. Comrade Bordiga and his faction of "Communist-Boycottists" (Comunista astensionista) are certainly wrong in advocating non-participation in parliament. But on one point, it seems to me, Comrade Bordiga is right — as far as can be judged from two issues of his paper, *Il Soviet* (Nos. 3 and 4, January 18 and February 1, 1920), from four issues of Comrade Serrati's excellent periodical, *Comunismo* (Nos. 1-4, October 1-November 30, 1919), and from isolated issues of Italian bourgeois papers which I have come across. Comrade Bordiga and his faction are right in attacking Turati and his followers, who remain in a party which has recognized Soviet power and the dictatorship of the proletariat, yet continue their former pernicious and opportunist policy as members of parliament. Of course, in tolerating this, Comrade Serrati and the whole Italian Socialist Party[21] are committing a mistake which threatens to do as much harm and give rise to the same dangers as it did in Hungary, where the Hungarian Turatis sabotaged both the Party and Soviet government from within. Such a mistaken, inconsistent, or spineless attitude towards the opportunist parliamentarians gives rise to "Left-wing" Communism, on the one hand, and *to a certain extent* justifies its existence, on the other. Comrade Serrati is obviously wrong when he accuses Deputy Turati of being "inconsistent" (*Comunismo*, No. 3), for it is precisely the Italian Socialist Party itself that is inconsistent in tolerating such opportunist parliamentarians as Turati and Co.

VIII

NO COMPROMISES?

In the quotation from the Frankfurt pamphlet we saw how emphatically the "Lefts" advance this slogan. It is sad to see people who doubtless consider themselves Marxists and want to be Marxists forgetting the fundamental truths of Marxism. This is what Engels — who, like Marx, was one of those rarest of authors whose every sentence in every one of their great works contains remarkably profound meaning — wrote in 1874 in opposition to the manifesto of the thirty-three Blanquist Communards:[22]

" 'We are Communists' (wrote the Blanquist Communards in their manifesto), 'because we want to attain our goal without stopping at intermediate stations, without any compromises, which only postpone the day of victory and prolong the period of slavery.'

"The German Communists are Communists because through all the intermediate stations and all compromises, created, not by them, but by the course of historical development, they clearly perceive and constantly pursue the final aim, viz., the abolition of classes and the creation of a society in which there will no longer be private ownership of land or of the means of production. The thirty-three Blanquists are Communists because they imagine that merely because *they* want to skip the intermediate stations and compromises, that settles the matter, and if 'it begins' in the next few days — which they take for granted — and they come to the helm, 'Communism will be introduced' the day after tomorrow. If that is not immediately possible, they are not Communists.

"What childish innocence it is to present impatience as a theoretically convincing argument!" (Fr. Engels, "Program of the Blanquist Communards,"[23] from the German Social-Democratic newspaper *Volksstaat*, 1874, No. 73, given in the Russian translation of *Articles, 1871-1875*, Petrograd, 1919, pp. 52-53.)

In the same article, Engels expresses his profound esteem for Vaillant, and speaks of the "undeniable merits" of the latter (who, like Guesde, was one of the most prominent leaders of international Socialism up to August 1914, when they both turned traitor to Socialism). But Engels does not allow an obvious mistake to pass without a detailed analysis. Of course, to very young and inexperienced revolutionaries, as well as to petty-bourgeois revolutionaries, of even a very respectable age and very experienced, it seems exceedingly "dangerous," incomprehensible and incorrect to "allow compromises." And many sophists (being unusually or excessively "experienced" politicians) reason exactly in the same way as the British leaders of opportunism mentioned by Comrade Lansbury: "If the Bolsheviks may make a certain compromise, why may we not make any kind of compromise?" But proletarians schooled in numerous strikes (to take only this manifestation of the class struggle) usually understand quite well the very profound (philosophical, historical, political and psychological) truth expounded by Engels. Every proletarian has been through strikes and has experienced "compromises" with the hated oppressors and exploiters, when the workers had to go back to work either without having achieved anything or agreeing to only a partial satisfaction of their demands. Every proletarian — owing to the conditions of the mass struggle and the sharp intensification of class antagonisms in which he lives — notices the difference between a compromise enforced by objective conditions (such as lack of strike funds, no outside support, extreme hunger and exhaustion), a compromise which in no way diminishes the revolutionary devotion and readiness for further struggle on the part of the workers who have agreed to such a compromise, and a compromise by traitors who try to ascribe to outside causes their own selfishness (strike-breakers also enter into "compromises"!), cowardice, desire to toady to the capitalists, and readiness to yield to intimidation, sometimes to persuasion, sometimes to sops, and sometimes to flattery on the part of the capitalists. (The history of the British labour movement offers especially many instances of such treacherous compromises by British trade union leaders, but, in one form or another, nearly all workers in all countries have witnessed the same sort of thing.)

Naturally, there are individual cases of exceptional difficulty and intricacy when the real character of this or that "compromise" can be correctly determined only with the greatest difficulty; just as there are cases of homicide where it is by no means easy to decide whether the homicide was fully justified and even necessary (as, for example, legitimate self-defence), or due to unpardonable negligence, or even to a cunningly executed perfidious plan. Of course, in politics, where it is sometimes a matter of extremely complicated — national and international — relations between classes and parties, very many cases will arise that will be much more difficult than the questions of a legitimate "compromise" in a strike, or the treacherous "compromise" of a strike-breaker, traitor leader, etc. It would be absurd to formulate a recipe or general rule ("No Compromises!") to serve all cases. One must use one's own brains and be able to find one's bearings in each separate case. That, in fact, is one of the functions of a party organization and of party leaders worthy of the title, namely, through the prolonged, persistent, variegated and comprehensive efforts of all thinking representatives of the given class,* to evolve the knowledge, the experience and — in addition to knowledge and experience — the political instinct necessary for the speedy and correct solution of intricate political problems.

Naive and utterly inexperienced people imagine that it is sufficient to admit the permissibility of compromises *in general* in order to obliterate the dividing line between opportunism, against which we wage and must wage an irreconcilable struggle, and revolutionary Marxism, or Communism. But if such people do not yet know that *all* dividing lines in nature and in society are mutable and to a certain extent conventional — they cannot be assisted otherwise than by a long process of training, education, enlightenment, and by political and everyday experience.   It is important to single out from the practical questions of the politics of each separate or specific historical moment those which reveal the principal type of impermissible, treacherous compromises, compromises embodying the opportunism that is fatal to the revolutionary class, and to exert all efforts to explain them and combat them.   During the imperialist war of 1914-18 between two groups of equally predatory and rapacious countries, the prin-

---

* Within every class, even in the conditions prevailing in the most enlightened countries, even within the most advanced class, and even when the circumstances of the moment have roused all its spiritual forces to an exceptional degree, there always are — and inevitably *will be* as long as classes exist, as long as classless society has not fully entrenched and consolidated itself, and has not developed on its own foundations — representatives of the class who do *not* think and are incapable of thinking.   Were this not so, capitalism would not be the oppressor of the masses it is.

cipal, fundamental type of opportunism was social-chauvinism, that is, support of "defence of the fatherland," which, in *such* a war, was really equivalent to defence of the predatory interests of one's "own" bourgeoisie. After the war, the defence of the robber "League of Nations," the defence of direct or indirect alliances with the bourgeoisie of one's own country against the revolutionary proletariat and the "Soviet" movement, and the defence of bourgeois democracy and bourgeois parliamentarism against "Soviet power" became the principal manifestations of those impermissible and treacherous compromises, the sum total of which constituted the opportunism that is fatal to the revolutionary proletariat and its cause.

"... One must emphatically reject all compromise with other parties ... all policy of manoeuvring and compromise,"

write the German Lefts in the Frankfurt pamphlet.

It is a wonder that, holding such views, these Lefts do not emphatically condemn Bolshevism! For the German Lefts must know that the whole history of Bolshevism, both before and after the October Revolution is *full* of instances of manoeuvring, temporizing and compromising with other parties, bourgeois parties included!

To carry on a war for the overthrow of the international bourgeoisie, a war which is a hundred times more difficult, protracted and complicated than the most stubborn of ordinary wars between states, and to refuse beforehand to manoeuvre, to utilize the conflict of interests (even though temporary) among one's enemies, to refuse to temporize and compromise with possible (even though temporary, unstable, vacillating and conditional) allies — is not this ridiculous in the extreme? Is it not as though, when making a difficult

66

ascent of an unexplored and heretofore inaccessible mountain, we were to refuse beforehand ever to move in zigzags, ever to retrace our steps, ever to abandon the course once selected and to try others? And yet we find that people so immature and inexperienced (if youth were the explanation, it would not be so bad; young people are ordained by god himself to talk such nonsense for a period) meet with the support — whether direct or indirect, open or covert, whole or partial, does not matter — of some members of the Communist Party of Holland!!

After the first socialist revolution of the proletariat, after the overthrow of the bourgeoisie in one country, the proletariat of that country *for a long time* remains *weaker* than the bourgeoisie, simply because of the latter's extensive international connections, and also because of the spontaneous and continuous restoration and regeneration of capitalism and the bourgeoisie by the small commodity producers of the country which has overthrown the bourgeoisie. The more powerful enemy can be vanquished only by exerting the utmost effort, and *without fail,* most thoroughly, carefully, attentively and skilfully using every, even the smallest, "rift" among the enemies, of every antagonism of interest among the bourgeoisie of the various countries and among the various groups or types of bourgeoisie within the various countries, and also by taking advantage of every, even the smallest, opportunity of gaining a mass ally, even though this ally be temporary, vacillating, unstable, unreliable and conditional. Those who fail to understand this, fail to understand even a particle of Marxism, or of scientific, modern Socialism *in general.* Those who have not proved by *deeds* over a fairly considerable period of time, and in fairly varied political situations, their ability to apply this truth in practice have not yet learned to assist the revolutionary class in its struggle to emancipate all toiling humanity from the exploiters. And this applies equally to the period *b e f o r e* and *a f t e r* the proletariat has conquered political power.

Our theory is not a dogma, but a *guide to action*,[24] said Marx and Engels; and it is the greatest mistake, the greatest crime on the part of such "patented" Marxists as Karl Kautsky, Otto Bauer, etc., that they have not understood this, have been unable to apply it at crucial moments of the proletarian revolution. "Political activity is not the pavement of the Nevsky Prospect"[25] (the clean, broad, smooth pavement of the perfectly straight principal street of St. Petersburg) — N. G. Chernyshevsky, the great Russian Socialist of the pre-Marxian period, used to say. Since Chernyshevsky's time Russian revolutionaries have paid the price of numerous sacrifices for ignoring or forgetting this truth. We must strive at all costs to *prevent* the Left Communists and the West-European and American revolutionaries who are devoted to the working class paying *as dearly* for the assimilation of this truth as the backward Russians did.

The Russian revolutionary Social-Democrats repeatedly utilized the services of the bourgeois liberals prior to the downfall of tsardom, that is, they concluded numerous practical compromises with them; and in 1901-02, even prior to the appearance of Bolshevism, the old editorial board of *Iskra* (consisting of Plekhanov, Axelrod, Zasulich, Martov, Potresov and myself) concluded (not for long, it is true) a formal political alliance with Struve, the political leader of bourgeois liberalism, while at the same time it was able to wage an unremitting and most merciless ideological and political struggle against bourgeois liberalism and against the slightest manifestation of its influence in the working-class movement.

68

The Bolsheviks have always adhered to this policy. Beginning with 1905, they systematically advocated an alliance between the working class and the peasantry against the liberal bourgeoisie and tsardom, never, however, refusing to support the bourgeoisie against tsardom (for instance, during second rounds of elections, or during second ballots) and never ceasing their relentless ideological and political struggle against the bourgeois revolutionary peasant party, the "Socialist-Revolutionaries," exposing them as petty-bourgeois democrats who falsely described themselves as Socialists. During the Duma elections in 1907, the Bolsheviks for a brief period entered into a formal political bloc with the "Socialist-Revolutionaries." Between 1903 and 1912 there were periods of several years in which we were formally united with the Mensheviks in one Social-Democratic Party; but we *never* ceased our ideological and political struggle against them as opportunists and vehicles of bourgeois influence among the proletariat. During the war we concluded certain compromises with the "Kautskyites," with the Left Mensheviks (Martov), and with a section of the "Socialist-Revolutionaries" (Chernov and Natanson); we were together with them at Zimmerwald and Kienthal and issued joint manifestoes; but we never ceased and never relaxed our ideological and political struggle against the "Kautskyites," Martov and Chernov (Natanson died in 1919 a "Revolutionary Communist" Narodnik, he was very close to and almost in agreement with us). At the very moment of the October Revolution we entered into an informal but very important (and very successful) political bloc with the petty-bourgeois peasantry by adopting the *Socialist-Revolutionary* agrarian program *in its entirety,* without a single alteration — that is, we effected an unquestionable compromise in order to prove to the peasants that we did not want to "steam-roller" them, but to reach agreement with them. At the same time we proposed (and soon after effected) a formal political bloc, including participation in the government, with the "Left Socialist-Revolutionaries," who dissolved this bloc after the conclusion of the Brest-Litovsk Peace and then, in July 1918, went to the length of armed rebellion, and subsequently of armed struggle, against us.

It is therefore understandable why attacks of the German Lefts on the Central Committee of the Communist Party of Germany for entertaining the idea of a bloc with the "Independents" (the "Independent Social-Democratic Party of Germany," the Kautskyites) appear to us to be utterly frivolous and a clear proof that the "Lefts" are in the *wrong*. We in Russia also had Right Mensheviks (who participated in the Kerensky government), corresponding to the German Scheidemanns, and Left Mensheviks (Martov), corresponding to the German Kautskyites, who were in opposition to the Right Mensheviks. A gradual shift of the worker masses from the Mensheviks to the Bolsheviks was to be clearly observed in 1917: at the First All-Russian Congress of Soviets, held in June 1917, we had only 13 per cent of the votes; the Socialist-Revolutionaries and the Mensheviks had the majority. At the Second Congress of Soviets (October 25, 1917) we had 51 per cent of the votes. Why is it that in Germany the *same* absolutely *identical* movement of the workers from Right to Left did not immediately strengthen the Communists, but first strengthened the intermediate "Independent" party, although this party never had independent political ideas or an independent policy, and only wavered between the Scheidemanns and the Communists?

Evidently, one of the reasons was the *mistaken* tactics of the German Communists, who must fearlessly and honestly admit this mistake and learn to rectify it. The mistake lay in their denial of the need to take part in the reactionary bourgeois parliaments and in the reactionary trade unions; the mistake lay in numerous manifestations of that "Left" infantile disorder which has now come to the surface and will consequently be cured more thoroughly, more quickly and with greater benefit to the organism.

The German "Independent Social-Democratic Party" is obviously not a homogeneous body: alongside the old opportunist leaders (Kautsky, Hilferding and, to a considerable extent, apparently, Crispien, Ledebour and others) — who have demonstrated their inability to understand the significance of Soviet power and the dictatorship of the proletariat, their inability to lead the revolutionary struggle of the proletariat — there has arisen in this party a Left, proletarian wing which is growing with remarkable rapidity. Hundreds of thousands of members of this party (which, it seems, has some three-quarters of a million members) are proletarians who are abandoning Scheidemann and are rapidly going towards Communism. This proletarian wing has already proposed — at the Leipzig (1919) Congress of the Independents — immediate and unconditional affiliation to the Third International. To fear a "compromise" with this wing of the party is positively ridiculous. On the contrary, it is *obligatory* for the Communists to seek *and to find* a suitable form of compromise with them, such a compromise as, on the one hand, would facilitate and accelerate the necessary complete fusion with this wing and, on the other, would in no way hamper the Communists in their ideological and political struggle against the opportunist Right wing of the "Independents." It will probably not be easy to devise a suitable form of compromise — but only a charlatan could promise the German workers and German Communists an "easy" road to victory.

Capitalism would not be capitalism if the "pure" proletariat were not surrounded by a large number of exceedingly motley types intermediate between the proletarian and the semi-proletarian (who earns his livelihood in part by the sale of his labour power), between the semi-proletarian and the small peasant (and petty artisan, handicraft worker and small master in general), between the small peasant and the middle peasant, and so on, and if the proletariat itself were not divided into more developed and less developed strata, if it were not divided according to territorial origin, trade, sometimes according to religion, and so on. And from all this follows the necessity, the absolute necessity, for the vanguard of the proletariat, for its class-conscious section, for the Communist Party, to resort to manoeuvres, arrangements and compromises with the various groups of proletarians, with the various parties of the workers and small masters. The whole point lies in *knowing how* to apply these tactics in order to *raise,* and not lower, the *general* level of proletarian class consciousness, revolutionary spirit, and ability to fight and win. Incidentally, it should be noted that the victory of the Bolsheviks over the Mensheviks demanded the application of tactics of manoeuvres, arrangements and compromises not only before *but also after* the October Revolution of 1917, but such manoeuvres and compromises, of course, as would assist, accelerate, consolidate and strengthen the Bolsheviks at the expense of the Mensheviks. The petty-bourgeois democrats (including the Mensheviks) inevitably vacillate between the bourgeoisie and the proletariat, between bourgeois democracy and the Soviet system, between reformism and revolutionism, between love-for-the-workers and fear of the proletarian dictatorship, etc. The proper tactics for the Communists must be to *utilize* these vacillations, not to ignore them; and utilizing them calls for concessions to those elements which are turning towards the proletariat — whenever and to the extent that they turn towards the proletariat — in addition to fighting those who turn towards the bourgeoisie. The result of the application of correct tactics is that Menshevism has disintegrated, and is disintegrating more and more in our country, that the stubbornly opportunist leaders are being isolated, and that the best of the workers and the best elements among the petty-bourgeois democrats are being brought into our camp. This is a long process, and the hasty "decision" — "No compromises, no manoeuvres" — can only injure the work of strengthening the influence of the revolutionary proletariat and enlarging its forces.

Lastly, one of the undoubted mistakes of the "Lefts" in Germany is their outright insistence on non-recognition of the Versailles Peace. The more "weightily" and "pompously," the more "emphatically" and dogmatically this viewpoint is formulated (by K. Horner, for instance), the less sensible does it appear. It is not enough, under the present conditions of the international proletarian revolution, to repudiate the preposterous absurdities of "National Bolshevism" (Lauffenberg and others), which has gone to the length of advocating a bloc with the German bourgeoisie for a war against the Entente. One must understand that the tactics of not admitting that it would be imperative for a Soviet Germany (if a German Soviet republic were to arise soon) to recognize the Versailles Peace for a time and to submit to it are funda-

73

mentally wrong. It does not follow from this that the "Independents" — at a time when the Scheidemanns were in the government, when Soviet government in Hungary had not yet been overthrown, and when the possibility of a Soviet revolution in Vienna supporting Soviet Hungary was not yet precluded — were right in putting forward, *under those circumstances,* the demand that the Versailles Peace be signed. At that time the "Independents" tacked and manoeuvred very clumsily, for they more or less accepted responsibility for the Scheidemann traitors and more or less sank from the level of advocating a merciless (and most cold-blooded) class war against the Scheidemanns to the level of advocating a "classless" or "above-class" standpoint.

But the position is now obviously such that the German Communists should not tie their hands and promise positively and categorically to repudiate the Versailles Peace in the event of the victory of Communism. That would be stupid. They must say: The Scheidemanns and the Kautskyites have perpetrated a number of acts of treachery which hindered (and in part directly ruined) the chances of an alliance with Soviet Russia and Soviet Hungary. We Communists will do all we can to *facilitate* and *pave the way* for such an alliance; and we are by no means obliged to repudiate the Versailles Peace, come what may, and, moreover, immediately. The possibility of repudiating it with success will depend not only on the German, but also on the international successes of the Soviet movement. The Scheidemanns and Kautskyites hampered this movement; we are helping it. That is the substance of the matter, that is where the fundamental difference lies. And if our class enemies, the exploiters and their lackeys, the Scheidemanns and Kautskyites, have missed many an opportunity for strengthening both the German and the international Soviet movement, of strengthening both the German and the international Soviet revolution, they are to blame. The Soviet revolution in Germany will strengthen the international Soviet movement, which is the strongest bulwark (and the only reliable, invincible and world-wide bulwark) against the Versailles Peace and against international imperialism in general. To give prime place absolutely, categorically and immediately to liberation from the Versailles Peace, to give it *precedence over the question* of liberating *other* countries oppressed by imperialism from the yoke of imperialism, is philistine nationalism (worthy of Kautsky, Hilferding, Otto Bauer and Co.) and not revolutionary internationalism. The overthrow of the bourgeoisie in any of the large European countries, including Germany, would be such a gain to the international revolution that for its sake one can, and if necessary should, tolerate a *more prolonged existence of the Versailles Peace*. If Russia, by herself, could endure the Brest-Litovsk Peace for several months to the advantage of the revolution, there is nothing impossible in a Soviet Germany, allied with Soviet Russia, enduring the existence of the Versailles Peace for a longer period to the advantage of the revolution.

The imperialists of France, England, etc., are trying to provoke the German Communists and to lay a trap for them: "Say that you will not sign the Versailles Peace!" And the Left Communists childishly fall into the trap laid for them, instead of skilfully manoeuvring against the crafty and, *at the present moment,* stronger enemy, and instead of telling him: "Now we will sign the Versailles Peace." To tie our hands beforehand, openly to tell the enemy, who is at present better armed than we are, whether we shall fight him, and when, is stupidity and not revolutionism. To accept battle at a time when it is obviously advantageous to the enemy and not to us is a crime; and the political leader of the revolutionary class who is unable to "tack, manoeuvre, and compromise" in order to avoid an obviously disadvantageous battle, is absolutely worthless.

IX

"LEFT-WING" COMMUNISM
IN GREAT BRITAIN

There is no Communist Party in Great Britain yet, but there is a fresh, broad, powerful and rapidly growing communist movement among the workers which justifies the brightest hopes. There are several political parties and organizations (the British Socialist Party,[26] the Socialist Labour Party, the South Wales Socialist Society, the Workers' Socialist Federation[27]) which desire to form a Communist Party and are already negotiating among themselves to this end. The *Workers' Dreadnought*, the weekly organ of the last of the organizations mentioned, in its issue of February 21, 1920, Vol. VI, No. 48, contains an article by the editor, Comrade Sylvia Pankhurst, entitled "Towards a Communist Party." The article outlines the progress of the negotiations between the four organizations mentioned for the formation of a united Communist Party, on the basis of affiliation to the Third International, the recognition of the Soviet system instead of parliamentarism, and the dictatorship of the proletariat. It appears that one of the greatest obstacles to the immediate formation of a united Communist Party is the disagreement over the question of participation in parliament and over the question whether the new Communist Party should affiliate to the old, trade unionist, opportunist and social-chauvinist Labour Party, which consists mostly of trade unions. The Workers' Socialist Federation and the Socialist Labour Party* are opposed to taking part in parliamentary elections and in parliament, and they are opposed to affiliation to the Labour Party; and in this they disagree with all, or with the majority, of the members of the British Socialist Party, which they regard as the "Right wing of the Communist Parties" in Great Britain. (Page 5, Sylvia Pankhurst's article.)

Thus, the main division is the same as in Germany, notwithstanding the enormous difference in the form in which the disagreements manifest themselves (in Germany the form is more analogous to the "Russian" than it is in Great Britain) and in a number of other things. Let us examine the arguments of the "Lefts."

On the question of participation in parliament, Comrade Sylvia Pankhurst refers to an article in the same issue by Comrade W. Gallacher, who writes in the name of the Scottish Workers' Council in Glasgow.

"The above council," he writes, "is definitely anti-parliamentarian, and has behind it the Left wing of the various political bodies. We represent the revolutionary movement in Scotland, striving continually to build up a revolutionary organization within the industries, and a Communist Party, based on social committees, throughout the country. For a considerable time we have been sparring with the official parliamentarians. We have not considered it necessary to declare open warfare on them, and they are *afraid* to open an attack on us.

"But this state of affairs cannot long continue. We are winning all along the line.

---

* I believe this party is opposed to affiliation to the Labour Party but not all its members are opposed to participation in parliament.

"The rank and file of the I.L.P. in Scotland is becoming more and more disgusted with the thought of Parliament, and Soviets (the Russian word transliterated into English is used) or workers' councils are being supported by almost every branch. This is very serious, of course, for the gentlemen who look to politics for a profession, and they are using any and every means to persuade their members to come back into the parliamentary fold. Revolutionary comrades *must not* (all italics are the author's) give any support to this gang. Our fight here is going to be a difficult one. One of the worst features of it will be the treachery of those whose personal ambition is a more impelling force than their regard for the revolution. Any support given to parliamentarism is simply assisting to put power into the hands of our British Scheidemanns and Noskes. Henderson, Clynes and Co. are hopelessly reactionary. The official I.L.P. is more and more coming under the control of middle class Liberals, who . . . have found their 'spiritual home' in the camp of Messrs. Mac-Donald, Snowden and Co. The official I.L.P. is bitterly hostile to the Third International, the rank and file is for it. Any support to the parliamentary opportunists is simply playing into the hands of the former. The B.S.P. doesn't count at all here. . . . What is wanted here is a sound revolutionary industrial organization, and a Communist Party working along clear, well-defined, scientific lines. If our comrades can assist us in building these, we will take their help gladly; if they cannot, for God's sake let them keep out altogether, lest they betray the revolution by lending their support to the reactionaries, who are so eagerly clamouring for parliamentary 'honours' (?) (the query mark is the author's) and who are so anxious to prove that they *can rule* as effectively as the 'boss' class politicians themselves."

This letter, in my opinion, excellently expresses the temper and point of view of the young Communists, or of rank-and-file workers who are only just coming to Communism. This temper is highly gratifying and valuable; we must learn to value it and to support it, for without it, it would be hopeless to expect the victory of the proletarian revolution in Great Britain, or in any other country for that matter. People who can give expression to this temper of the masses, who can rouse such a temper (which is very often dormant, unrealized and unaroused) among the masses, must be valued and

79

every assistance must be given them.   And at the same time we must openly and frankly tell them that temper *alone* is not enough to lead the masses in a great revolutionary struggle, and that such and such mistakes that very loyal adherents of the cause of the revolution are about to commit, or are committing, may damage the cause of the revolution.   Comrade Gallacher's letter undoubtedly betrays the germs of *all* the mistakes that are being committed by the German "Left" Communists and that were committed by the Russian "Left" Bolsheviks in 1908 and 1918.

The writer of the letter is imbued with a noble, proletarian hatred for the bourgeois "class politicians" (a hatred understood and shared, however, not only by the proletarian but by all working people, by all "small folk," to use a German expression). This hatred of a representative of the oppressed and exploited masses is verily the "beginning of all wisdom," the basis of every socialist and communist movement and of its success.   But the writer apparently does not appreciate that politics is a science and an art that does not drop from the skies, that it is not obtained gratis, and that the proletariat, if it wants to conquer the bourgeoisie, must train its *own,* proletarian "class politicians," and such as will be no worse than the bourgeois politicians.

The writer of the letter is perfectly clear in the point that only workers' Soviets, and not parliament, can be the instrument whereby the aims of the proletariat will be achieved. And, of course, those who have failed to understand this up to now are inveterate reactionaries, even if they are most highly educated people, most experienced politicians, most sincere Socialists, most erudite Marxists, and most honest citizens and family men.   But the writer of the letter does not even ask, it does not occur to him to ask, whether it is possible to bring about the victory of the Soviets over parliament without getting pro-Soviet politicians *into* parliament, without disintegrating parliamentarism from *within,* without working within parliament for the success of the Soviets in their forthcoming task of dispersing parliament. And yet the writer of the letter expresses the absolutely correct idea that the Communist Party in Great Britain must act on *scientific* principles. Science demands, firstly, that the experience of other countries be taken into account, especially if these other, also capitalist, countries are undergoing, or have recently undergone, a very similar experience; secondly, it demands that account be taken of *all* the forces, groups, parties, classes and masses operating in the given country, and that policy should not be determined only by the desires and views, by the degree of class consciousness, and the readiness for battle of only one group or party.

That the Hendersons, the Clynes, the MacDonalds and the Snowdens are hopelessly reactionary is true. It is equally true that they want to take power in their own hands (though they prefer a coalition with the bourgeoisie), that they want to "rule" on the old bourgeois lines, and that when they do get into power they will unfailingly behave like the Scheidemanns and Noskes. All that is true. But it by no means follows that to support them is treachery to the revolution, but rather that in the interests of the revolution the working-class revolutionaries should give these gentlemen a certain amount of parliamentary support. To explain this idea I shall take two contemporary British political documents: 1) the speech delivered by the Prime Minister, Lloyd George, on March 18, 1920 (reported in the *Manchester Guardian* of March 19, 1920) and 2) the arguments of a "Left" Communist, Comrade Sylvia Pankhurst, in the article mentioned above.

Arguing against Asquith (who was especially invited to this meeting but declined to attend) and against those Liberals who want not a coalition with the Conservatives, but closer relations with the Labour Party (Comrade Gallacher, in his letter, also points to the fact that Liberals are joining the Independent Labour Party), Lloyd George said that a coalition, and a *close* coalition at that, between the Liberals and Conservatives was essential, otherwise there might be a victory for the Labour Party, which Lloyd George "prefers to call" Socialist and which is striving for the "collective ownership" of the means of production. "In France this was called Communism," the leader of the British bourgeoisie said, putting it popularly for his auditors, the Liberal members of Parliament, who probably had not known it before, "in Germany it was called Socialism, and in Russia it is called Bolshevism." To Liberals this is unacceptable on principle, explained Lloyd George, because they stand in principle for private property. "Civilization is in danger," declared the speaker, and, therefore, the Liberals and the Conservatives must unite....

". . . If you go to the agricultural areas," said Lloyd George, "I agree that you have the old party divisions as strong as ever. They are removed from the danger. It does not walk their lanes. But when they see it they will be as strong as some of those industrial constituencies are now. Four-fifths of this country is industrial and commercial; hardly one-fifth is agricultural. It is one of the things I have constantly in my mind when I think of the dangers of the future here. In France the population is agricultural, and you have a solid body of opinion which does not move very rapidly, and which is not very easily excited by revolutionary movements. That is not the case here. This country is more top-heavy than any country in the world, and if it begins to rock, the crash here, for that reason, will be greater than in any land."

From this the reader will see that Mr. Lloyd George is not only a very clever man, but that he has also learned a great deal from the Marxists. It would be no sin for us to learn something from Lloyd George.

It is interesting to note the following episode which occurred in the course of the discussion that followed Lloyd George's speech:

"Mr. Wallace, M.P.: I should like to ask what the Prime Minister considers the effect might be in the industrial constituencies upon the industrial workers, so many of whom are Liberals at the present time and from whom we get so much support. Would not a possible result be to cause an immediate overwhelming accession of strength to the Labour Party from men who at present are our cordial supporters?

"The Prime Minister: I take a totally different view. The fact that Liberals are fighting among themselves undoubtedly drives a very considerable number of Liberals in despair to the Labour Party, where you get a considerable body of Liberals, very able men, whose business it is to discredit the Government. The result is undoubtedly to bring a good accession of public sentiment to the Labour Party. It does not go to the Liberals who are outside, it goes to the Labour Party, the by-elections show that."

It may be said in passing, that this argument shows in particular how muddled even the cleverest members of the bourgeoisie have become and how they cannot help committing irreparable stupidities. That in fact will cause the downfall of the bourgeoisie. But our people may commit stupidities (provided, of course, that they are not too serious and are rectified in time) and yet in the long run come out the victors.

The second political document is the following argument advanced by a "Left" Communist, Comrade Sylvia Pankhurst:

". . . Comrade Inkpin (the General Secretary of the British Socialist Party) refers to the Labour Party as 'the main body of the working-class movement.' Another comrade of the British Socialist Party, at the conference of the Third International, just held, put the British Socialist

Party position more strongly. He said: 'We regard the Labour Party as the organized working class.'

"We do not take this view of the Labour Party. The Labour Party is very large numerically, though its membership is to a great extent quiescent and apathetic, consisting of men and women who have joined the trade unions because their workmates are trade unionists, and to share the friendly benefits.

"But we recognize that the great size of the Labour Party is also due to the fact that it is the creation of a school of thought beyond which the majority of the British working class has not yet emerged, though great changes are at work in the mind of the people which will presently alter this state of affairs. . . .

"The British Labour Party, like the social patriotic organizations of other countries, will, in the natural development of society, inevitably come into power. It is for the Communists to build up the forces that will overthrow the social patriots, and in this country we must not delay or falter in that work.

"We must not dissipate our energy in adding to the strength of the Labour Party; its rise to power is inevitable. We must concentrate on making a communist movement that will vanquish it. The Labour Party will soon be forming a government; the revolutionary opposition must make ready to attack it. . . ."

Thus the liberal bourgeoisie is abandoning the historical system of "two parties" (of exploiters) which has been hallowed by age-long experience and which has been extremely advantageous to the exploiters, and considers it necessary to unite their forces to combat the Labour Party. A number of the Liberals are deserting to the Labour Party like rats from a sinking ship. The Left Communists believe that the transfer of power to the Labour Party is inevitable and admit that at present it has the support of the majority of the workers. From this they draw the strange conclusion which Comrade Sylvia Pankhurst formulates as follows:

"The Communist Party must not compromise. . . . The Communist Party must keep its doctrine pure, and its independence of reformism inviolate; its mission is to lead the way, without stopping or turning, by the direct road to the communist revolution."

On the contrary, from the fact that the majority of the workers in Great Britain still follow the lead of the British Kerenskys or Scheidemanns and have not yet had the experience of a government composed of these people, which experience was required in Russia and Germany to secure the mass passage of the workers to Communism, it undoubtedly follows that the British Communists *should* participate in parliamentary action, that they should, from *within* parliament, help the masses of the workers to see the results of a Henderson and Snowden government in practice, that they should help the Hendersons and Snowdens to defeat the united forces of Lloyd George and Churchill. To act otherwise would mean placing difficulties in the way of the revolution; for revolution is impossible without a change in the views of the majority of the working class, and this change is brought about by the political experience of the masses, and never by propaganda alone. "To lead the way without compromises, without stopping or turning" — if this is said by an obviously impotent minority of the workers which knows (or at all events should know) that if Henderson and Snowden gain the victory over Lloyd George and Churchill, the majority will in a brief space of time become disappointed in their leaders and will begin to support Communism (or at all events will adopt an attitude of neutrality, and for the most part of benevolent neutrality, towards the Communists), then this slogan is obviously mistaken. It is just as if 10,000 soldiers were to fling themselves into battle against 50,000 enemy soldiers, when the thing to do would have been to "stop," to "turn," or even to effect a "compromise" to gain time until the arrival of the 100,000 reinforcements which were on their way but which could not go into action immediately. That is the childishness of the intellectual and not the serious tactics of a revolutionary class.

The fundamental law of revolution, which has been confirmed by all revolutions, and particularly by all three Russian revolutions in the twentieth century, is as follows: it is not enough for revolution that the exploited and oppressed masses should understand the impossibility of living in the old way and demand changes; it is essential for revolution that the exploiters should not be able to live and rule in the old way. Only when the *"lower classes" do not want* the old way, and when the "upper classes" *cannot carry on in the old way* — only then can revolution triumph. This truth may be expressed in other words: revolution is impossible without a nation-wide crisis (affecting both the exploited and the exploiters). It follows that for revolution it is essential, first, that a majority of the workers (or at least a majority of the class-conscious, thinking, politically active workers) should fully understand that revolution is necessary and be ready to sacrifice their lives for it; secondly, that the ruling classes should be passing through a governmental crisis, which draws even the most backward masses into politics (a symptom of every real revolution is a rapid, tenfold and even hundredfold increase in the number of members of the toiling and oppressed masses — hitherto apathetic — who are capable of waging the political struggle), weakens the government and makes it possible for the revolutionaries to overthrow it rapidly.

In Great Britain, as can be seen, among other things, from Lloyd George's speech, both conditions for a successful proletarian revolution are clearly maturing. And the mistakes of the Left Communists are particularly dangerous at the present time precisely because certain revolutionaries are not displaying a sufficiently thoughtful, sufficiently attentive, sufficiently intelligent and sufficiently shrewd interest in each of these conditions. If we are the party of the revolutionary *class*, and not a revolutionary group, if we want the *masses* to follow us (and unless we do, we stand the risk of remaining mere windbags), we must, firstly, help Henderson or Snowden to beat Lloyd George and Churchill (or, rather, compel the former to beat the latter, because the former *are afraid of their victory*!); secondly, we must help the majority of the working class to convince themselves by their own experience that we are right, that is, that the Hendersons and Snowdens are absolutely unsuitable, that they are petty bourgeois and treacherous by nature, and that their bankruptcy is inevitable; thirdly, we must bring nearer the moment when, *on the basis* of the disappointment of the majority of the workers in the Hendersons, it will be possible with serious chances of success to overthrow the government of the Hendersons at once; because if that most astute and solid big bourgeois, not petty bourgeois, Lloyd George, is betraying utter consternation and is more and more weakening himself (and the bourgeoisie as a whole) by his "friction" with Churchill one day and his "friction" with Asquith the next, how much greater will be the consternation of a Henderson government!

I will put it more concretely. In my opinion, the British Communists should unite their four (all very weak, and some very, very weak) parties and groups into a single Communist Party on the basis of the principles of the Third International and of *obligatory* participation in parliament. The Communist Party should propose a "compromise" to the Hendersons and Snowdens, an election agreement: let us together fight the alliance of Lloyd George and the Conservatives, let us divide the parliamentary seats in proportion to the number of votes cast by the workers for the Labour Party and for the Communist Party (not at the elections, but in a special vote), and let us retain *complete liberty* of agitation, propaganda and political activity. Without this latter condition, of course, we cannot agree to a bloc, for it would be treachery; the British Communists must absolutely insist on and secure complete liberty to expose the Hendersons and the Snowdens in the same way as (*for fifteen years,* 1903-17) the Russian Bolsheviks insisted on and secured it in relation to the Russian Hendersons and Snowdens, i.e., the Mensheviks.

If the Hendersons and the Snowdens consent to a bloc on these terms, we shall be the gainers, because the number of parliamentary seats is of no importance to us; we are not out for seats, we will yield on this point (the Hendersons, on the other hand, and particularly their new friends — or new masters — the Liberals who have joined the Independent Labour Party are most anxious to get seats). We shall be the gainers, because we shall carry *our* agitation among the *masses* at a time when Lloyd George *himself* has "incensed" them, and we shall not only help the Labour Party to establish its government more quickly, but also help the masses to understand more quickly the communist propaganda that we shall carry on against the Hendersons without any curtailment or omission.

If the Hendersons and the Snowdens reject a bloc with us on these terms we shall gain still more, for we shall have at once shown the *masses* (note that even in the purely Menshevik and utterly opportunist Independent Labour Party the *masses* are for Soviets) that the Hendersons prefer *their* close relations with the capitalists to the unity of all the workers. We shall immediately gain in the eyes of the *masses,* who, particularly after the brilliant, highly correct and highly useful (for Communism) explanations given by Lloyd George, will sympathize with the idea of uniting all the workers against the Lloyd George-Conservative alliance. We shall gain immediately because we shall have demonstrated to the masses that the Hendersons and the Snowdens are afraid to beat Lloyd George, are afraid to take power alone, and are striving *secretly* to secure the support of Lloyd George, who is *openly* extending his hand to the Conservatives against the Labour Party. It should be noted that in Russia, after the revolution of February 27, 1917 (old style), the propaganda of the Bolsheviks against the Mensheviks and Socialist-Revolutionaries (i.e., the Russian Hendersons and Snowdens) benefited precisely because of a circumstance of this kind. We said to the Mensheviks and the Socialist-Revolutionaries: take over the entire power without the bourgeoisie, because you have a majority in the Soviets (at the First All-Russian Congress of Soviets, in June 1917, the Bolsheviks had only 13 per cent of the votes). But the Russian Hendersons and Snowdens feared to take power without the bourgeoisie, and when the bourgeoisie delayed the elections to the Constituent Assembly, knowing perfectly well that the elections would give a majority to the Socialist-Revolutionaries and the Mensheviks* (who had a close

* The result of the elections to the Constituent Assembly in Russia in November 1917, based on returns embracing over 36,000,000 voters, were as follows: the Bolsheviks obtained 25 per cent of the votes; the various parties of the landlords and bourgeoisie obtained 13 per cent, and the petty-bourgeois democratic parties, i.e., the Socialist-Revolutionaries, Mensheviks and a number of small kindred groups, obtained 62 per cent.

political bloc and actually represented *one and the same* petty-bourgeois democracy), the Socialist-Revolutionaries and Mensheviks were unable energetically and consistently to oppose these delays.

If the Hendersons and the Snowdens reject a bloc with the Communists, the Communists will gain immediately as regards winning the sympathy of the masses and discrediting the Hendersons and Snowdens; and if as a result we do lose a few parliamentary seats, it is a matter of no importance to us. We would put up our candidates in a very few but absolutely safe constituencies, namely, constituencies where putting up our candidate would not give the seat to the Liberal and lose it for the Labour candidate. We would take part in the election campaign, distribute leaflets in favour of Communism, and, in *all* constituencies where we have no candidates, we would urge the electors *to vote for the Labour candidate and against the bourgeois candidate.* Comrades Sylvia Pankhurst and Gallacher are mistaken in thinking that this is a betrayal of Communism, or a renunciation of the struggle against the social traitors. On the contrary, the cause of communist revolution would undoubtedly gain by it.

At present the British Communists very often find it hard to approach the masses and even to get a hearing from them. If I come out as a Communist and call upon the workers to vote for Henderson against Lloyd George, they will certainly give me a hearing. And I will be able to explain in a popular manner not only why Soviets are better than parliament and why the dictatorship of the proletariat is better than the dictatorship of Churchill (disguised by the signboard of bourgeois "democracy"), but also that I want with my vote to support Henderson in the same way as the rope supports a hanged man — that the impending establishment of a government of Hendersons will prove that I am right, will bring the masses over to my side, and will hasten the political death of the Hendersons and the Snowdens just as was the case with their kindred spirits in Russia and Germany.

And if the objection is raised that these tactics are too "subtle," or too complicated, that the masses will not understand them, that these tactics will split and scatter our forces, will prevent us concentrating them on the Soviet revolution, etc., I will reply to the "Lefts" who raise this objection: don't ascribe your doctrinairism to the masses! The masses in Russia are probably no better educated than the masses in England; if anything, they are less so. Yet the masses understood the Bolsheviks; and the fact that *on the eve* of the Soviet revolution, in September 1917, the Bolsheviks put up their candidates for a bourgeois parliament (the Constituent Assembly) and *on the morrow* of the Soviet revolution, in November 1917, took part in the elections to this Constituent Assembly, which they dispersed on January 5, 1918 — this did not hamper the Bolsheviks, but on the contrary, helped them.

I cannot deal here with the second point of disagreement among the British Communists — the question of affiliating or not affiliating to the Labour Party. I have too little material at my disposal on this question, which is a particularly complex one in view of the quite unique character of the British Labour Party, the very structure of which is so unlike the political parties common to the Continent. It is beyond doubt, however, first, that on this question, too, those who try to deduce the tactics of the revolutionary proletariat from principles like: "The Communist Party must keep its doctrine pure, and its independence of reform-ism inviolate; its mission is to lead the way, without stop-ping or turning, by the direct road to the communist revolu-tion" — will inevitably fall into error. For such principles are merely a repetition of the mistakes committed by the French Blanquist Communards, who, in 1874, "repudiated" all compromises and all intermediate stations. Secondly, it is beyond doubt that in this question too, as always, the task is to learn to apply the general and basic principles of Communism to the *peculiar* relations between classes and parties, to the *peculiar features* of the objective develop-ment towards Communism which are characteristic of each country and which must be studied, discovered, divined.

But this must be discussed not in connection with British Communism alone, but in connection with the general con-clusions concerning the development of Communism in all capitalist countries. We shall now proceed to deal with this theme.

X

SOME CONCLUSIONS

The Russian bourgeois revolution of 1905 revealed a very peculiar turn in world history: in one of the most backward capitalist countries the strike movement attained a breadth and power without precedent anywhere in the world. In the *first month of 1905 alone* the number of strikers was over ten times the *annual* average for the previous ten years (1895-1904); and from January to October 1905 strikes grew continuously and reached enormous dimensions. Under the influence of a number of entirely unique historical conditions, backward Russia was the first to show the world not only the growth, by leaps and bounds, of the independent activity of the oppressed masses in time of revolution (this had occurred in all great revolutions), but also a significance of the proletariat infinitely exceeding the numerical ratio of the latter to the total population, a combination of the economic strike and the political strike, the transformation of the latter into armed uprising, and the birth of a new form of mass struggle and mass organization of the classes oppressed by capitalism, viz., the Soviets.

The revolutions of February and October 1917 led to the all-round development of the Soviets on a national scale, and to their victory in the proletarian, socialist revolution. And in less than two years there became revealed the international character of the Soviets, the spread of this form of struggle and organization to the world working-class movement, and the historical mission of the Soviets as the grave-digger, heir and successor of bourgeois parliamentarism, and of bourgeois democracy in general.

More. The history of the working-class movement now shows that in all countries it is about to experience (and has already begun to experience) a struggle between Communism, which is growing, gaining strength and marching towards victory, and, first and foremost, its *own* (in each country) "Menshevism," i.e., opportunism and social-chauvinism, and, secondly — as a supplement so to say — "Left-wing" Communism. The former struggle has developed in all countries, apparently without a single exception, as a struggle between the Second International (already virtually killed) and the Third International. The latter struggle can be observed in Germany, Great Britain, Italy, America (at any rate, a certain *section* of the Industrial Workers of the World and the anarcho-syndicalist trends uphold the errors of Left-wing Communism side by side with an almost universal and undivided acceptance of the Soviet system) and France (the attitude of a section of the former syndicalists towards the political party and parliamentarism, again side by side with the acceptance of the Soviet system), in other words, the struggle is undoubtedly being waged not only on an international, but even on a world-wide scale.

But while the working-class movement is everywhere passing through what is actually the same kind of preparatory school for victory over the bourgeoisie, it is in each country achieving this development in *its own way*. The big, advanced capitalist countries are marching along this road *much more rapidly* than did Bolshevism, which history granted fifteen years to prepare itself, as an organized political trend, for victory. In the short space of one year, the Third International has already scored a decisive victory; it has defeated the Second, yellow, social-chauvinist International, which only a few months ago was incomparably stronger than the Third International, seemed to be stable and powerful and enjoyed the all-round support — direct and indirect, material (Cabinet posts, passports, the press) and ideological — of the world bourgeoisie.

The whole point now is that the Communists of every country should quite consciously take into account both the main fundamental tasks of the struggle against opportunism and "Left" doctrinairism and the *specific features* which this struggle assumes and inevitably must assume in each separate country in conformity with the peculiar features of its economics, politics, culture, national composition (Ireland, etc.), its colonies, religious divisions, and so on and so forth. Everywhere we can feel that dissatisfaction with the Second International is spreading and growing, both because of its opportunism and because of its inability, or incapacity, to create a really centralized, a really leading centre that would be capable of directing the international tactics of the revolutionary proletariat in its struggle for a world Soviet republic. We must clearly realize that such a leading centre cannot under any circumstances be built up on stereotyped, mechanically equalized and identical tactical rules of struggle. As long as national and state differences exist among peoples and countries — and these differences will continue to exist for a very long time even after the dictatorship of the proletariat has been established on a world scale — the unity of international tactics of the Communist working-class movement of all countries demands, not the elimination of variety, not the abolition of national differences (that is a foolish dream at the present moment), but such an application of the *fundamental* principles of Communism (Soviet power and the dictatorship of the proletariat) as will *correctly modify* these principles in certain *particulars,* correctly adapt and apply them to national and national-state differences. Investigate, study, seek, divine, grasp that which is peculiarly national, specifically national in the *concrete manner* in which each country approaches the fulfilment of the *single* international task, in which it approaches the victory over opportunism and "Left" doctrinairism within the working-class movement, the overthrow of the bourgeoisie, and the establishment of a Soviet republic and a proletarian dictatorship — such is the main task of the historical period through which all the advanced countries (and not only the advanced countries) are now passing. The main thing — not everything by a very long way, of course, but the main thing — has already been achieved in that the vanguard of the working class has been won over, in that it has ranged itself on the side of Soviet government against parliamentarism, on the side of the dictatorship of the proletariat against bourgeois democracy. Now all efforts, all attention, must be concentrated on the *next* step — which seems, and from a certain standpoint really is — less fundamental, but which, on the other hand, is actually closer to the practical carrying out of the task, namely: seeking the forms of *transition* or *approach* to the proletarian revolution.

The proletarian vanguard has been won over ideologically. That is the main thing. Without this not even the first step towards victory can be made. But it is still a fairly long way from victory. Victory cannot be won with the vanguard alone. To throw the vanguard alone into the decisive battle, before the whole class, before the broad masses have taken up a position either of direct support of the vanguard, or at least of benevolent neutrality towards it, and one in which they cannot possibly support the enemy, would be not merely folly but a crime. And in order that actually the whole class, that actually the broad masses of the working people and those oppressed by capital may take up such a position, propaganda and agitation alone are not enough. For this the masses must have their own political experience. Such is the fundamental law of all great revolutions, now confirmed with astonishing force and vividness not only in Russia but also in Germany. Not only the uncultured, often illiterate, masses of Russia, but the highly cultured, entirely literate masses of Germany had to realize through their own painful experience the absolute impotence and spinelessness, the absolute helplessness and servility to the bourgeoisie, the utter vileness of the government of the knights of the Second International, the absolute inevitability of a dictatorship of the extreme reactionaries (Kornilov in Russia, Kapp and Co. in Germany) as the only alternative to a dictatorship of the proletariat, in order to turn them resolutely toward Communism.

The immediate task that confronts the class-conscious vanguard of the international labour movement, i.e., the Communist parties, groups and trends, is to be able *to lead* the broad masses (now, for the most part, slumbering, apathetic, bound by routine, inert and dormant) to their new position, or, rather, to be able to lead *not only* their own party, but also these masses, in their approach, their transition to the new position. While the first historical task (that of winning over the class-conscious vanguard of the proletariat to Soviet power and the dictatorship of the working class) could not be accomplished without a complete ideological and political victory over opportunism and social-chauvinism, the second task, which now becomes the immediate task, and which consists in being able to lead the *masses* to the new position that can ensure the victory of the vanguard in the revolution — this immediate task cannot be accomplished without eliminating Left doctrinairism, without completely overcoming and eliminating its mistakes.

As long as the question was (and in so far as it still is) one of winning over the vanguard of the proletariat to Communism, so long, and to that extent, propaganda was in the forefront; even propaganda circles, with all the defects of the circle spirit, are useful under these conditions and produce fruitful results. But when it is a question of practical action by the masses, of the disposition, if one may so express it, of vast armies, of the alignment of *all* the class forces of the given society *for the final and decisive battle,* then propaganda habits alone, the mere repetition of the truths of "pure" Communism, are of no avail. In these circumstances one must not count in thousands, as the propagandist does who belongs to a small group that has not yet given leadership to the masses; in these circumstances one must count in millions and tens of millions. In these circumstances we must not only ask ourselves whether we have convinced the vanguard of the revolutionary class, but also whether the historically effective forces of *all* classes — positively of all the classes of the given society without exception — are aligned in such a way that everything is fully ripe for the decisive battle; in such a way that 1) all the class forces hostile to us have become sufficiently entangled, are sufficiently at loggerheads with each other, have sufficiently weakened themselves in a struggle which is beyond their strength; that 2) all the vacillating, wavering, unstable, intermediate elements — the petty bourgeoisie and the petty-bourgeois democrats as distinct from the bourgeoisie — have sufficiently exposed themselves in the eyes of the people, have sufficiently disgraced themselves through their practical bankruptcy; and that 3) among the proletariat a mass sentiment in favour of supporting the most determined, supremely bold, revolutionary action against the bourgeoisie has arisen and begun vigorously to grow. Then revolution is indeed ripe; then, indeed, if we have correctly gauged all the conditions indicated and briefly outlined above, and if we have chosen the moment rightly, our victory is assured.

The divergences between the Churchills and the Lloyd Georges — with insignificant national differences these political types exist in *all* countries — on the one hand, and between the Hendersons and the Lloyd Georges on the other, are quite minor and unimportant from the standpoint of pure, i.e., abstract Communism, i.e., Communism that has not yet matured to the stage of practical, mass, political action. But from the standpoint of this practical action by the masses, these differences are very, very important. To take account of these differences, to determine the moment when the inevitable conflicts between these "friends" which weaken and enfeeble *all the "friends" taken together* will have completely matured — that is the crux of the matter, the whole task of the Communist who wants to be not merely a class-conscious and convinced propagandist of ideas, but a practical leader of the *masses* in the revolution. The strictest devotion to the ideas of Communism must be combined with the ability to effect all the necessary practical compromises, to manoeuvre, to make agreements, zigzags, retreats and so on, in order to accelerate the coming to, and loss of, political power by the Hendersons (the heroes of the Second International, if we are to speak not of individuals, the representatives of petty-bourgeois democracy who call themselves Socialists); to accelerate their inevitable bankruptcy in practice, which will enlighten the masses precisely in the spirit of our ideas, in the direction of Communism; to accelerate the inevitable friction, quarrels, conflicts and utter discord between the Hendersons, the Lloyd Georges and the Churchills (the Mensheviks and Socialist-Revolutionaries, the Constitutional-Democrats and the monarchists; the Scheidemanns, the bourgeoisie and the Kappists, etc.); and to select the proper moment when the discord among these "pillars of sacred private property" is at its height, in order, by a determined offensive of the proletariat, to defeat them all and capture political power.

History generally, and the history of revolutions in particular, is always richer in content, more varied, more many-sided, more lively and "subtle" than even the best parties and the most class-conscious vanguards of the most advanced classes imagine. This is understandable, because even the best vanguards express the class consciousness, will, passion and imagination of tens of thousands; whereas revolutions are made, at moments of particular upsurge and the exertion of all human capacities, by the class consciousness, will, passion and imagination of tens of millions, spurred on by a most acute struggle of classes. From this follow two very important practical conclusions: first, that in order to fulfil its task the revolutionary class must be able to master *all* forms, or aspects, of social activity without any exception (completing, after the capture of political power, sometimes at great risk and very great danger, what it did not complete before the capture of power); second, that the revolutionary class must be ready to pass from one form to another in the quickest and most unexpected manner.

Everyone will agree that an army which does not train itself to wield all arms, all the means and methods of warfare that the enemy possesses or may possess, behaves in an unwise or even in a criminal manner. But this applies to politics even more than it does to war. In politics it is even harder to forecast what methods of warfare will be applicable and advantageous to us under specific future conditions. Unless we master all means of warfare, we may suffer grave, often even decisive, defeat if changes beyond our control in the position of the other classes bring to the forefront forms of activity in which we are particularly weak. If, however, we master all means of warfare, victory will be certain, because we represent the interests of the really foremost and really revolutionary class, even if circumstances do not permit us to bring into play the weapons that are most dangerous to the enemy, weapons that deal the swiftest mortal blows. Inexperienced revolutionaries often think that legal methods of struggle are opportunist because in this field the bourgeoisie has especially frequently (particularly in "peaceful," non-revolutionary times) deceived and fooled the workers, and that illegal methods of struggle are revolutionary. But that is not true. What is true is that those parties and leaders are opportunists and traitors to the working class who are unable or unwilling (don't say you cannot, say you will not!) to apply illegal methods of struggle in conditions such as those which prevailed, for example, during the imperialist war of 1914-18, when the bourgeoisie of the freest democratic countries deceived the workers in the most insolent and brutal manner, forbidding the truth to be told about the predatory character of the war. But revolutionaries who are unable to combine illegal forms of struggle with *every* form of legal struggle are poor revolutionaries indeed. It is not difficult to be a revolutionary when revolution has already broken out and is at its height, when everybody is joining the revolution just because they are carried away, because it is the fashion, and sometimes even out of careerist motives. After its victory, the proletariat has to make most strenuous efforts, to suffer the pains of martyrdom, one might say, to "liberate" itself from such pseudo revolutionaries. It is far more difficult — and of far greater value — to be a revolutionary when the conditions for direct, open, really mass and really revolutionary struggle *do not yet exist,* to be able to champion the interests of the revolution (by propaganda, agitation and organization) in non-revolutionary bodies and often enough in downright reactionary bodies, in a non-revolutionary situation, among masses who are incapable of immediately appreciating the need for revolutionary methods of action. To be able to find, to probe for, to correctly determine the specific path or the particular turn of events that will *lead* the masses to the real, last, decisive, and great revolutionary struggle — such is the main task of Communism in Western Europe and America today.

Great Britain offers an example. We cannot tell, and no one can tell beforehand, how soon a real proletarian revolution will flare up there, and *what immediate cause* will most serve to rouse, kindle, and impel into the struggle the very wide masses who are at present dormant. Hence, it is our duty to carry on all our preparatory work in such a way, as to be well shod on all four feet (as the late Plekhanov, when he was a Marxist and revolutionary, was fond of saying). It is possible that the "breach" will be forced, "the ice broken" by a parliamentary crisis, or by a crisis arising out of the colonial and imperialist contradictions, which are hopelessly entangled and are becoming increasingly painful and acute, or perhaps by some third cause, etc. We are not discussing the kind of struggle that will *determine* the fate of the proletarian revolution in Great Britain (not a single Communist has any doubt on that score; for all of us this question is settled, and settled definitely); what we are discussing is the *immediate cause* that will bring into motion the at present dormant proletarian masses and lead them directly to revolution. Let us not forget that in the French bourgeois republic, for example, in a situation which from both the international and national aspect was a hundred times less revolutionary than the present, such an "unexpected" and "petty" immediate cause as one of the many thousands of fraudulent tricks of the reactionary military caste (the Dreyfus case[28]), was enough to bring the people to the verge of civil war!

The Communists in Great Britain should constantly, unremittingly and undeviatingly utilize parliamentary elections and all the vicissitudes of the Irish, colonial and world imperialist policy of the British government, and all other fields, spheres and facets of public life, and work, in all of them in a new way, in a communist way, in the spirit of the Third, and not of the Second, International. I have neither the time nor the space here to describe the "Russian," "Bolshevik" methods of participation in parliamentary elections and in the parliamentary struggle; but I can assure the foreign Communists that it was totally unlike the usual West-European parliamentary campaigns. From this the conclusion is often drawn: "Well, that was in Russia; in our country parliamentarism is different." A wrong conclusion. But it is just why Communists, adherents of the Third International in all countries exist — to *change*, all along the line, in all spheres of life, the old socialist, trade unionist, syndicalist, parliamentary work into *new* work, communist work. In Russia, too, there was always a great deal of opportunist and purely bourgeois commercialism and capitalist swindling in the elections. The Communists in Western Europe and America must learn to create a new, unusual, non-opportunist, non-careerist parliamentarism; the Communist parties must issue their slogans; real proletarians, with the help of the unorganized and downtrodden poor, should scatter and distribute leaflets, canvass workers' houses and the cottages of the rural proletarians and peasants in the remote villages (fortunately there are many times less remote villages in Europe than in Russia, and in England the number is very small); they should go into the most common taverns, penetrate into the unions, societies and casual meetings where the common people gather, and talk to the people, not in learned (and not in very parliamentary) language; they should not at all strive to "get seats" in parliament, but should everywhere strive to rouse the minds of the masses and draw them into the struggle, to hold the bourgeoisie to its word and utilize the apparatus it has set up, the elections it has appointed, the appeals it has made to the whole people, and to tell the people what Bolshevism is in a way that has never been possible (under bourgeois rule) outside of election times (not counting, of course, times of big strikes, when, in Russia, a *similar* apparatus for widespread popular agitation worked even more intensively). It is very difficult to do this in Western Europe and America, very, very difficult; but it can and must be done, for the task of Communism cannot be fulfilled without effort; and our efforts must be devoted to fulfilling *practical* tasks, ever more varied, ever more closely connected with all branches of social life, *winning* branch after branch and sphere after sphere *from the bourgeoisie*.

In Great Britain, further, the work of propaganda, agitation and organization among the armed forces and among the oppressed and unfranchised nationalities in one's "*own*" state (Ireland, the colonies) must also be taken up in a new way (not in a socialist, but a communist way, not in a reformist, but a revolutionary way). Because in the era of imperialism generally, and especially now, after the war, which was a torment to the peoples and quickly opened their eyes to the truth (viz., that tens of millions were killed and maimed only for the purpose of deciding whether the British or the German pirates should plunder the largest number of countries), all these spheres of social life are being especially charged with inflammable material and are creating numerous causes of conflicts, crises and the accentuation of the class struggle. We do not and cannot know which spark — of the innumerable sparks that are flying around in all countries as a result of the economic and political world crisis — will kindle the conflagration, in the sense of specially rousing the masses, and we must, therefore, with the aid of our new, communist principles, set to work to "stir up" all and sundry, even the oldest, mustiest and seemingly hopeless spheres, for otherwise we shall not be able to cope with our tasks, we shall not be comprehensively prepared, we shall not master all arms and we shall not prepare ourselves to achieve either the victory over the bourgeoisie (which arranged all sides of social life — and has now disarranged them — in its bourgeois way) or the impending communist reorganization of every sphere of life after that victory.

After the proletarian revolution in Russia and its victories on an international scale, which were unexpected for the bourgeoisie and the philistines, the whole world has changed, and the bourgeoisie has changed everywhere too. It is terrified of "Bolshevism," incensed with it almost to the point of frenzy, and, precisely for that reason, it is, on the one hand, accelerating the progress of events and, on the other, concentrating attention on the suppression of Bolshevism by force, and thereby weakening its position in a number of other fields. The Communists in all advanced countries must take into account both these circumstances in their tactics.

When the Russian Cadets and Kerensky launched a furious campaign against the Bolsheviks — especially after April 1917, and more particularly in June and July 1917 — they "overdid" it. Millions of copies of bourgeois papers, shrieking in every key against the Bolsheviks, helped to induce the masses to appraise Bolshevism; and, apart from the newspapers, all public life was being permeated with discussions about Bolshevism just because of the "zeal" of the bourgeoisie. Now on an international scale the millionaires of all countries are behaving in a way that deserves our heartiest thanks. They are hounding Bolshevism with the same zeal as did Kerensky and Co.; they, too, are "overdoing" it and *helping* us just as Kerensky did. When the French bourgeoisie makes Bolshevism the central issue at the elections, and accuses the comparatively moderate or vacillating Socialists of being Bolsheviks; when the American bourgeoisie, having completely lost its head, seizes thousands and thousands of people on suspicion of Bolshevism, creates an atmosphere of panic and broadcasts stories of Bolshevik plots; when the British bourgeoisie — the most "solid" in the world — despite all its wisdom and experience, commits incredible follies, founds richly endowed "anti-Bolshevik societies," creates a special literature on Bolshevism, and hires an extra number of scientists, agitators and parsons to combat it — we must bow and thank the capitalist gentry. They are working for us. They are helping us to get the masses interested in the nature and significance of Bolshevism. And they cannot do otherwise; for they have *already* failed to stifle Bolshevism, to "ignore" it.

But at the same time, the bourgeoisie sees practically only one side of Bolshevism, viz., insurrection, violence, terror; it therefore strives to prepare itself for resistance and opposition particularly in *this* field. It is possible that in certain instances, in certain countries, and for certain brief periods, it will succeed in this. We must reckon with such a possibility, and there will be absolutely nothing terrible for us if it does succeed. Communism "springs" from positively every sphere of public life; its shoots are to be seen literally everywhere. The "contagion" (to use the favourite metaphor of the bourgeoisie and the bourgeois police, the one most "pleasant" to them) has very thoroughly permeated the organism and has completely impregnated it. If special efforts are made to "stop up" one of the channels, the "contagion" will find another, sometimes a very unexpected channel. Life will assert itself. Let the bourgeoisie rave, work itself into a frenzy, go to extremes, commit follies, take vengeance on the

Bolsheviks in advance, and endeavour to kill off (in India, Hungary, Germany, etc.) more hundreds, thousands, and hundreds of thousands of yesterday's and tomorrow's Bolsheviks. In acting thus, the bourgeoisie is acting as all classes doomed by history have acted. Communists should know that the future in any case belongs to them; therefore, we can (and must) combine the most intense passion in the great revolutionary struggle with the coolest and most sober estimation of the frenzied ravings of the bourgeoisie. The Russian revolution was cruelly defeated in 1905; the Russian Bolsheviks were defeated in July 1917; over 15,000 German Communists were killed as a result of the wily provocation and cunning manoeuvres of Scheidemann and Noske working hand in glove with the bourgeoisie and the monarchist generals; White terror is raging in Finland and Hungary. But in all cases and in all countries Communism is becoming steeled and is growing; its roots are so deep that persecution does not weaken it, does not debilitate it, but strengthens it. Only one thing is lacking to enable us to march forward more confidently and firmly to victory, namely, the universal and thoroughly thought-out appreciation by all Communists in all countries of the necessity of displaying the utmost *flexibility* in their tactics. The communist movement, which is developing magnificently, especially in the advanced countries, now lacks this appreciation and the ability to apply it in practice.

What happened to such leaders of the Second International, such highly erudite Marxists devoted to Socialism as Kautsky, Otto Bauer and others, could (and should) serve as a useful lesson. They fully appreciated the need for flexible tactics; they learned themselves and taught others Marxist dialectics (and much of what they have done in this respect will forever remain a valuable contribution to socialist literature); but *in the application* of these dialectics they committed such a mistake, or proved in practice to be so *un*dialectical, so incapable of taking into account the rapid change of forms and the rapid acquiring of new content by the old forms, that their fate is not much more enviable than that of Hyndman, Guesde and Plekhanov.

The principal reason for their bankruptcy was that they were "enchanted" by one definite form of growth of the working-class movement and Socialism, they forgot all about the one-sidedness of this form, they were afraid of seeing the sharp break which objective conditions made inevitable, and continued to repeat simple, routine, and, at a first glance, incontestable truths, such as: "three is more than two." But politics is more like algebra than arithmetic; and still more like higher mathematics than elementary mathematics. In reality, all the old forms of the socialist movement have acquired a new content, and, consequently, a new sign, the "minus" sign, has appeared in front of all the figures; but our wiseacres stubbornly continued (and still continue) to persuade themselves and others that "minus three" is more than "minus two"!

We must see to it that Communists do not make the same mistake, only the other way round; or, rather, we must see to it that the *same mistake,* only the other way round, made by the "Left" Communists, is corrected as soon as possible and overcome as quickly and painlessly as possible. It is not only Right doctrinairism that is a mistake; Left doctrinairism is also a mistake. Of course, the mistake of Left doctrinairism in Communism is at present a thousand times less dangerous and less significant than the mistakes of Right doctrinairism (i.e., social-chauvinism and Kautskyism); but, after all, that is only due to the fact that Left Communism is a very young trend, is only just coming into being. It is only for this reason that, under certain conditions, the disease can be easily cured; and we must set to work to cure it with the utmost energy.

The old forms have burst asunder, for it has turned out that their new content — an anti-proletarian and reactionary content — had attained inordinate development. Today our work has, from the standpoint of the development of international Communism, such a durable, strong and powerful content (for Soviet power, for the dictatorship of the proletariat) that it can *and must* manifest itself in every form, both new and old, it can and must regenerate, conquer and subjugate all forms, not only the new, but also the old — not for the purpose of reconciling itself with the old, but for the purpose of making all and every form — new and old — a weapon for the complete, final, decisive and irrevocable victory of Communism.

The Communists must exert every effort to direct the working-class movement and social development in general along the straightest and quickest road to the universal victory of Soviet power and the dictatorship of the proletariat. That is an incontestable truth. But it is enough to take one little step further — a step that might seem to be in the same direction — and truth becomes error. We have only to say, as the German and British Left Communists say, that we recognized only one road, only the direct road, that we will not permit tacking, manoeuvring, compromising — and it will be a mistake which may cause, and in part has already caused, and is causing, very serious harm to Communism. Right doctrinairism persisted in recognizing only the old forms, and became utterly bankrupt, for it did not perceive the new content.   Left doctrinairism persists in the unconditional repudiation of certain old forms, failing to see that the new content is forcing its way through all and sundry forms, that it is our duty as Communists to master all forms, to learn how, with the maximum rapidity, to supplement one form with another, to substitute one for another, and to adapt our tactics to every such change called forth not by our class, nor by our efforts.

World revolution has received such a powerful impetus and acceleration from the horrors, atrocities and abominations of the world imperialist war and from the hopelessness of the situation it created — this revolution is developing in breadth and depth with such magnificent rapidity, with such a splendid variety of changing forms, with such an instructive, practical refutation of all doctrinairism, that there is every ground for hoping for a rapid and complete recovery of the international communist movement from the infantile disorder of "Left-wing" Communism.

April 27, 1920

Before publishing houses in our country — which has been plundered by the imperialists of the whole world in revenge for the proletarian revolution, and which is still being plundered and blockaded by them regardless of all promises they made to their workers — had succeeded in getting out my pamphlet, additional material arrived from abroad. Without claiming to present in my pamphlet anything more than the cursory notes of a publicist, I shall touch briefly upon a few points.

I

THE SPLIT AMONG THE GERMAN COMMUNISTS

The split among the Communists in Germany has become an accomplished fact. The "Lefts," or the "opposition on principle," have formed a separate "Communist Labour Party," as distinct from the "Communist Party." Apparently, a split is also imminent in Italy — I say apparently, as I have only two additional issues (Nos. 7 and 8) of the Left newspaper, *Il Soviet,* in which the possibility and necessity of a split is openly discussed, and mention is also made of a congress of the "Abstentionist" faction (or the boycottists, i.e., opponents of participation in parliament), which faction is still a part of the Italian Socialist Party.

There is reason to fear that the split with the "Lefts," the anti-parliamentarians (in part also anti-politicals, the opponents of a political party and of work in the trade unions) will become an international phenomenon, like the split with the "Centrists" (or Kautskyites, Longuetites, "Independents," etc.). Be it so. At all events, a split is better than confusion which impedes the ideological, theoretical and revolutionary growth and maturing of the party and its harmonious, really organized practical work which actually paves the way for the dictatorship of the proletariat.

Let the "Lefts" put themselves to a practical test on a national and international scale; let them try to prepare for (and then realize) the dictatorship of the proletariat without a strictly centralized party with an iron discipline, without the ability to master every sphere, every branch, every variety of political and cultural work. Practical experience will soon make them wiser.

But every effort must be made to prevent the split with the "Lefts" from impeding, or to see that it impedes as little as possible, the necessary amalgamation into a single party — which is inevitable in the near future — of all those in the working-class movement who sincerely and conscientiously stand for Soviet government and the dictatorship of the proletariat. It was the exceptional fortune of the Bolsheviks in Russia to have fifteen years in which to wage a systematic and thorough struggle both against the Mensheviks (that is, the opportunists and "Centrists") and against the "Lefts," long before the direct mass struggle for the dictatorship of the proletariat began. In Europe and America the same work has to be done now by "forced marches." Certain individuals, especially among the unsuccessful claimants to leadership, may (if they lack proletarian discipline and are not "honest with themselves") persist in their mistakes for a long time; but when the time is ripe the masses of the workers will easily and quickly unite themselves and unite all sincere Communists to form a single party capable of establishing the Soviet system and the dictatorship of the proletariat.*

---

* With regard to the question of the future amalgamation of the "Left" Communists, the anti-parliamentarians, with the Communists in general, I would make the following additional remarks. As far as I have been able to familiarize myself with the newspapers of the "Left" Communists and with those of the Communists in general in Germany, I find that the former have the advantage of being better able to carry on agitation among the masses than the latter. I have repeatedly observed something similar to this in the history of the Bolshevik Party, though on a smaller scale and in individual local organizations and not on a national scale. For instance, in 1907-08 the "Left" Bolsheviks on certain occasions and in certain places carried on more successful agitation among the masses than we did. This may be partly due to the fact that at a revolutionary moment, or at a time when revolutionary recollections are still fresh, it is easier to approach the masses with tactics of "mere" negation. This, however, is not an argument proving the correctness of such tactics. At all events there is not the least doubt that a Communist *Party* which wishes to be the real vanguard, the advanced detachment of the revolutionary *class,* the proletariat, and which, in addition, wishes to learn to lead the broad *masses* — not only the proletarian, but also the *non*-proletarian masses of toilers and exploited — must know how to conduct propaganda, how to organize, and how to carry on agitation in a manner most accessible, most comprehensible, most clear and vivid both to the urban, factory masses and to the rural masses.

II

THE COMMUNISTS AND THE INDEPENDENTS
IN GERMANY

I have expressed the opinion in this pamphlet that a compromise between the Communists and the Left wing of the Independents is necessary and useful to Communism, but that it will not be easy to effect. The newspapers which I have subsequently received have confirmed this opinion on both points. No. 32 of *The Red Flag*, the organ of the Central Committee of the Communist Party of Germany (*Die Rote Fahne*, Zentralorgan der Kommunistischen Partei Deutschlands — Spartacusbund — of March 26, 1920), published a "statement" of this Central Committee on the Kapp-Luttwitz military putsch[29] (conspiracy, adventure) and on the "socialist government." This statement is quite correct both as to its basic premise and its practical conclusions. The basic premise is that at the present moment there is no "objective basis" for the dictatorship of the proletariat because "the majority of the urban workers" support the Independents. The conclusion is — a promise to be a "loyal opposition" (i.e., renunciation of preparations for a "violent overthrow") to a "socialist government if it excludes bourgeois-capitalist parties."

Undoubtedly, these tactics are in the main correct. And though there is no need to dwell on minor inexactitudes of formulation, we cannot refrain from saying that a government of social traitors cannot be described (in an official statement of the Communist Party) as a "socialist" government; that one cannot speak of the exclusion of "bourgeois-capitalist parties," when the parties both of the Scheidemanns and of Messrs. the Kautskys and Crispiens are petty bourgeois-democratic parties; that it is impermissible to write such things as are contained in paragraph 4 of the statement, which reads:

> ". . . For the further winning of the proletarian masses for Communism, a state of things where political freedom could be utilized without restraint, and where bourgeois democracy could not manifest itself as a dictatorship of capital is of the greatest importance from the standpoint of the development of the proletarian dictatorship. . . ."

Such a state of things is impossible. Petty-bourgeois leaders, the German Hendersons (Scheidemanns) and Snowdens (Crispiens), do not and cannot go beyond the bounds of bourgeois democracy, which, in its turn, cannot but be the dictatorship of capital. There was no need at all to write such things, which are wrong in principle and harmful politically, for the attainment of the practical results for which the Central Committee of the Communist Party had been quite rightly striving. It would have been sufficient to say (if one wished to observe parliamentary amenities) that as long as the majority of the urban workers follow the Independents, we Communists must do nothing to prevent these workers overcoming their last philistine-democratic (i.e., also "bourgeois-capitalist") illusions by going through the experience of having their "own" government. That is sufficient ground for a compromise which is really necessary, and should consist in renouncing for a certain period all attempts at the violent overthrow of a government which enjoys the confidence of a majority of the urban workers. But in everyday mass agitation, in which one is not bound by official parliamentary amenities, one might, of course, add: Let rascals like the Scheidemanns, and philistines like the Kautskys and Crispiens reveal by their deeds how they have been fooled themselves and how they are fooling the workers; their "clean" government will itself do the "cleanest" job of all in "cleaning" the Augean stables[30] of Socialism, Social-Democracy and other forms of social treachery.

The real nature of the present leaders of the Independent Social-Democratic Party of Germany (those of whom it is wrongly said that they have already lost all influence, whereas, in reality, they are even more dangerous to the proletariat than the Hungarian Social-Democrats who styled themselves Communists and promised to "support" the dictatorship of the proletariat) was revealed once again during the German Kornilov affair, i.e., the Kapp-Luttwitz putsch.* A small but striking illustration is afforded by two brief articles — one by Karl Kautsky entitled "Decisive Hours" ("Entscheidende Stunden") in *Freiheit* (*Freedom*, the organ of the Independents) of March 30, 1920, and the other by Arthur Crispien entitled "On the Political Situation" (in this same newspaper, issue of April 14, 1920). These gentlemen are absolutely incapable of thinking and reasoning like revolutionaries. They are snivelling philistine democrats, who become a thousand times more dangerous to the proletariat when they claim to be supporters of Soviet government and of the dictatorship of the proletariat, because actually whenever a difficult and dangerous situation arises they are sure to commit treachery . . . while "sincerely" believing that they are helping the proletariat! Did not the Hungarian Social-Democrats, having rechristened themselves Communists, also want to "help" the proletariat when, owing to their cowardice and spinelessness, they considered the situation of

---

* Incidentally, this has been dealt with in an exceptionally clear, concise, exact and Marxist way in the excellent organ of the Austrian Communist Party, *The Red Flag*, of March 28 and 30, 1920 (*Die Rote Fahne*, Wien, 1920, Nos. 266 and 267; L.L.: "Ein neuer Abschnitt der deutschen Revolution" ["A New Stage of the German Revolution"]).

the Soviet system in Hungary hopeless and went snivelling to the agents of the Entente capitalists and the Entente hangmen?

III
TURATI AND CO. IN ITALY

The issues of the Italian newspaper *Il Soviet* referred to above, fully confirm what I have said in the pamphlet about the error committed by the Italian Socialist Party in tolerating such members and even such a group of parliamentarians in its ranks. It is still further confirmed by such an outside observer as the Rome correspondent of the English bourgeois-liberal newspaper, the *Manchester Guardian* whose interview with Turati is published in that paper on March 12, 1920. This correspondent writes:

". . . Signor Turati's opinion is that the revolutionary peril is not such as to cause undue anxiety in Italy. The Maximalists are fanning the fire of Soviet theories only to keep the masses awake and excited. These theories are, however, merely legendary notions, unripe programs incapable of being put to practical use. They are likely only to maintain the working classes in a state of expectation. The very men who use them as a lure to dazzle proletarian eyes find themselves compelled to fight a daily battle for the extortion of some often trifling economic advantages so as to delay the moment when the working classes will lose their illusions and faith in their cherished myths. Hence a long string of strikes of all sizes and with all pretexts up to the very latest one in the mail and railway services — strikes which make the already hard conditions of the country still worse. The country is irritated owing to the difficulties connected with its Adriatic problem, is weighed down by its foreign debt and by its inflated paper circulation, and yet it is still far from realizing the necessity of adopting that discipline of work which alone can restore order and prosperity. . . ."

It is clear as daylight that this English correspondent has blurted out the truth, which is in all probability being concealed and glossed over by Turati himself and his bourgeois defenders, accomplices and inspirers in Italy. This truth is that the ideas and political activities of Messrs. Turati, Treves, Modigliani, Dugoni and Co. are really and precisely such as are described by the English correspondent. It is downright social treachery. Just look at this advocacy of order and discipline among the workers, who are wage slaves toiling to enrich the capitalists! And how familiar to us Russians all these Menshevik speeches are! What a valuable admission it is that the masses are *for* Soviet government! How stupid and vulgarly bourgeois is the failure to understand the revolutionary role of spontaneously spreading strikes! Yes, indeed, the correspondent of the English bourgeois-liberal newspaper has rendered a backhanded service to Messrs. Turati and Co., and has excellently confirmed the correctness of the demand of Comrade Bordiga and his friends of *Il Soviet*, who are insisting that the Italian Socialist Party, if it really wants to be *for* the Third International, should drum Messrs. Turati and Co. out of its ranks and become a Communist Party both in name and in deeds.

IV

INCORRECT CONCLUSIONS FROM CORRECT PREMISES

But Comrade Bordiga and his "Left" friends draw from their correct criticism of Messrs. Turati and Co. the wrong conclusion that participation in parliament is harmful in general. The Italian "Lefts" cannot advance even a shadow of serious argument in support of this view. They simply do not know (or try to forget) the international examples of really revolutionary and communist utilization of bourgeois parliament which has been of unquestionable value in preparing for the proletarian revolution. They simply cannot conceive of a "new" way of utilizing parliament, and keep shouting and endlessly repeating themselves about the "old," non-Bolshevik way.

This is precisely where their fundamental mistake lies. Not only in the parliamentary field, but in *all* fields of activity Communism *must introduce* (and without long, persistent and stubborn effort it will be *unable* to introduce) something new in principle that will represent a radical break with the traditions of the Second International (while retaining and developing what was good in the latter).

Let us take, say, journalistic work. Newspapers, pamphlets and leaflets perform a necessary work of propaganda, agitation and organization. Not a single mass movement in any at all civilized country can dispense with a journalistic apparatus. No outcries against "leaders," no solemn vows to preserve the purity of the masses from the influence of leaders will obviate the necessity of utilizing for this work people who come from a bourgeois intellectual environment or will get rid of the bourgeois-democratic, "private property" atmosphere and environment in which this work is performed under capitalism. Even two and a half years after the overthrow of the bourgeoisie, after the conquest of political power by the proletariat, we still have this atmosphere around us, this mass (peasant, artisan) environment of bourgeois-democratic private-property relations.

Parliamentarism is one form of activity, journalism is another. The content of both can be communist, and it should be communist if those engaged in both spheres are real Communists, are real members of a proletarian mass party. Yet, in neither sphere — nor *in any other sphere of activity* under capitalism and during the period of transition from capitalism to Socialism — is it possible to avoid those difficulties which the proletariat must overcome, those special problems which the proletariat must solve in order to utilize for its own purposes the services of those who have come from the ranks of the bourgeoisie, in order to gain the victory over bourgeois intellectual prejudices and influences, in order to weaken the resistance of (and, ultimately, completely to transform) the petty-bourgeois environment.

Did we not, before the war of 1914-18, witness in all countries an extraordinary abundance of instances of extreme "Left" anarchists, syndicalists and others fulminating against parliamentarism, deriding bourgeois-vulgarized parliamentary Socialists, castigating their careerism, and so on and so forth, and yet themselves making the *same kind* of bourgeois career *through* journalism and *through* work in the syndicates (trade unions)? Are not the examples of Messrs. Jouhaux and Merrheim, to limit oneself to France, typical?

The childishness of those who "repudiate" participation in parliament consists precisely in the fact that they think it possible to "*solve*" the difficult problem of combating bourgeois-democratic influences *within* the working-class movement by such a "simple," "easy," supposedly revolutionary method, when in reality they are only running away from their own shadow, only closing their eyes to difficulties and only trying to brush them aside with mere words. The most shameless careerism, bourgeois utilization of parliamentary seats, glaring reformist perversion of parliamentary activity, vulgar, petty-bourgeois routine are all unquestionably common and prevalent characteristic features that are engendered by capitalism everywhere, not only outside but also inside the working-class movement. But then capitalism, and the bourgeois environment it creates (which disappears very slowly even after the overthrow of the bourgeoisie, for the peasantry constantly regenerates the bourgeoisie), give rise to what is also essentially bourgeois careerism, national chauvinism, petty-bourgeois vulgarity, etc., only varying insignificantly in form — in positively every sphere of activity and life.

You think, my dear boycottists and anti-parliamentarians, that you are "terribly revolutionary," but in reality *you are frightened* by the comparatively small difficulties of the struggle against bourgeois influences within the working-class movement, whereas your victory — i.e., the overthrow of the bourgeoisie and the conquest of political power by the proletariat — will create *these very same* difficulties on a still larger, an infinitely larger scale. Like children, you are frightened by a small difficulty which confronts you today, not understanding that tomorrow and the day after you will have to learn just the same, and learn thoroughly, to overcome the same difficulties, only on an immeasurably greater scale.

Under Soviet rule, your proletarian party and ours will be invaded by a still larger number of bourgeois intellectuals. They will worm their way into the Soviets, the courts, and the administration, for Communism cannot be built otherwise than with the aid of the human material created by capitalism, and the bourgeois intellectuals cannot be expelled and destroyed, but must be vanquished, remoulded, assimilated and re-educated, just as we must — in a protracted struggle waged on the basis of the dictatorship of the proletariat — re-educate the proletarians themselves, who do not abandon their petty-bourgeois prejudices at one stroke, by a miracle, at the behest of the Virgin Mary, at the behest of a slogan, resolution or decree, but only in the course of a long and difficult mass struggle against mass petty-bourgeois influences. Under Soviet rule these same problems, which the anti-parliamentarians are now so proudly, so haughtily, so lightly and so childishly brushing aside with a wave of the hand — *these very same* problems are arising anew *within* the Soviets, within the Soviet administration, among the Soviet "attorneys" (in Russia we have abolished, and have rightly abolished, the bourgeois legal bar, but it is reviving again under the guise of the "Soviet" "attorneys"[31]). Among the Soviet engineers, the Soviet schoolteachers and the privileged, i.e., the most highly skilled and best situated, *workers* in the Soviet factories, we observe a constant revival of absolutely *all* the negative traits peculiar to bourgeois parliamentarism, and we are conquering this evil — gradually — only by tireless, constant, prolonged and persistent struggle, proletarian organization and discipline.

Of course, under the rule of the bourgeoisie it is very "difficult" to eradicate bourgeois habits from our own, i.e., the workers' party; it is "difficult" to expel from the Party the habitual parliamentary leader who has been hopelessly corrupted by bourgeois prejudices; it is "difficult" to subject to proletarian discipline the absolutely essential (even if very limited) number of people coming from the ranks of the bourgeoisie; it is "difficult" to form in a bourgeois parliament a communist group fully worthy of the working class; it is "difficult" to ensure that the communist parlia-

123

mentarians do not play the bourgeois parliamentary game of skittles, but concern themselves with the very urgent work of propaganda, agitation and organization among the masses. All this is "difficult," to be sure; it was difficult in Russia, and it is incomparably more difficult in Western Europe and America, where the bourgeoisie is far stronger, where bourgeois-democratic traditions are stronger, and so on.

Yet all these "difficulties" are mere child's play compared with precisely *the same sort* of problems which in any event the proletariat will inevitably have to solve in order to achieve victory, both during the proletarian revolution and after the seizure of power by the proletariat. Compared with *these* truly gigantic problems of re-educating, under the proletarian dictatorship, millions of peasants and small masters, hundreds of thousands of office employees, officials and bourgeois intellectuals, of subordinating them all to the proletarian state and to proletarian leadership, of vanquishing their bourgeois habits and traditions — compared with these gigantic problems it is childishly easy to establish, under the rule of the bourgeoisie, in a bourgeois parliament, a really communist group of a real proletarian party.

If our "Left" and anti-parliamentarian comrades do not learn to overcome even such a small difficulty now, we may safely assert that either they will prove incapable of achieving the dictatorship of the proletariat, will be unable to subordinate and remould the bourgeois intellectuals and bourgeois institutions on a wide scale, or they will have *to complete their education in great haste*, and by this haste will do a great deal of harm to the cause of the proletariat, they will commit more errors than usual, will manifest more than the average weakness and inefficiency, and so on and so forth.

As long as the bourgeoisie has not been overthrown, and after that as long as small-scale economy and small commodity production have not entirely disappeared, the bourgeois atmosphere, proprietary habits and petty-bourgeois traditions will hamper proletarian work both outside and inside the working-class movement, not only in one field of activity, parliamentary, but inevitably in every field of social activity, in all cultural and political spheres without exception. And the attempt to brush aside, to fence oneself off from *one* of the "unpleasant" problems or difficulties in one sphere of activity is a profound mistake, which will later most certainly have to be paid for. We must study and learn how to master every sphere of work and activity without exception, to overcome all difficulties and all bourgeois habits, customs and traditions everywhere. Any other way of presenting the question is just trifling, just childishness.

May 12, 1920

V

In the Russian edition of this book I somewhat incorrectly described the conduct of the Communist Party of Holland as a whole in the sphere of international revolutionary policy. I therefore avail myself of the present opportunity to publish a letter from our Dutch comrades on this question and to correct the expression "Dutch Tribunists," which I used in the Russian text, and for which I now substitute the words "some members of the Communist Party of Holland."

N. Lenin

LETTER FROM WYNKOOP

Moscow, July 30, 1920

Dear Comrade Lenin,

Thanks to your kindness, we members of the Dutch delegation to the Second Congress of the Communist International were able to read your *"Left-Wing" Communism, an Infantile Disorder* prior to its publication in the European languages. In several places in the book you emphasize your disapproval of the part played by some members of the Communist Party of Holland in international politics.

We feel, nevertheless, that we must protest against your laying the responsibility for their actions on the Communist Party. This is extremely inaccurate. More, it is unjust, because these members of the Communist Party of Holland take little or no part in the Party's current activities and are endeavouring, directly or indirectly, to implement in the Communist Party of Holland opposition slogans against which the Party and all its organs have waged, and continue to wage to this day, a most energetic struggle.

Fraternally yours,
(on behalf of the
Dutch delegation)
D. I. Wynkoop

Written in April-May 1920

*First published in pamphlet
form in June 1920*

NOTES

[1] Lenin wrote *"Left-Wing" Communism, an Infantile Disorder* in April 1920 and the Appendix on May 12, 1920. The pamphlet appeared in Russian, June 8-10, 1920, and then in German, French and English in July. Lenin personally read the pamphlet's page proofs and machine proofs to ensure publication in time for the Second Congress of the Communist International. The pamphlet was circulated to all the Congress delegates. Between July and November 1920, a German edition appeared in Leipzig, a French edition in Paris, and an English one in London.

The manuscript of *"Left-Wing" Communism* bore the sub-title: "Popular Exposition of Marxist Strategy and Tactics," which was omitted in all the editions brought out during Lenin's lifetime. The present translation follows the first Russian edition, the proofs of which were checked by Lenin.   p. 1

[2] The reference is to the shooting of the workers of the Lena gold fields in Siberia by tsarist troops in April 1912. The Lena workers had gone on strike in protest against brutal exploitation by the management. Workers in all parts of Russia replied to the Lena shooting by mass political strikes and demonstrations which ushered in a new powerful rise of the revolutionary working-class movement.   p. 12

[3] *Longuetism* — a Centrist trend within the French Socialist Party headed by Jean Longuet.

The Longuetites took a social-pacifist stand in the First World War. Following the victory of the Great October Socialist Revolution in Russia, they proclaimed their support for the dictatorship of the proletariat, but in actual fact remained hostile to it, continuing their policy of reconciliation with the social-chauvinists and supporting the predatory Peace of

Versailles. In December 1920 the Longuetites, together with the avowed reformists, broke away from the French Socialist Party and affiliated to the so-called Two-and-a-Half International, and after the disintegration of that body returned to the Second International. p. 13

[4] *The Independent Labour Party* was formed in 1893 and was led by Keir Hardie, Ramsay MacDonald, and others. It claimed to be politically independent of the bourgeois parties; actually it was "independent of Socialism, but dependent upon liberalism" (Lenin). p. 13

[5] *Fabians* — members of the reformist and opportunist Fabian Society, formed by a group of British bourgeois intellectuals in 1884. The society took its name from the Roman General Fabius Cunctator (the "Delayer"), famous for his procrastinating tactics and avoidance of decisive battles. The Fabian Society represented, as Lenin put it, "the most finished expression of opportunism and liberal-labour politics." The Fabians sought to deflect the proletariat from the class struggle and advocated the possibility of a peaceful, gradual transition from capitalism to socialism by means of reforms. During the imperialist world war (1914-18) the Fabians took a social-chauvinist stand. For a characterization of the Fabians, see Lenin's "Preface to the Russian Edition of *Letters by J. F. Becker, J. Dietzgen, F. Engels, K. Marx and Others to F. A. Sorge and Others*" (V. I. Lenin, *Marx-Engels-Marxism,* Moscow, 1953, pp. 245-46), "The Agrarian Program of Social-Democracy in the Russian Revolution" (*Collected Works,* 4th Russ. ed., Vol. XV, p. 154), and "English Pacifism and English Dislike of Theory" (*ibid.,* Vol. XXI, p. 234). p. 13

[6] *The German Independent Social-Democratic Party* — a Centrist party formed in April 1917.
The party split at its Halle Congress in October 1920, and in December of that year a considerable part of its membership united with the Communist Party of Germany. The Right wing formed a separate party which existed under the old name, Independent Social-Democratic Party, until 1922, when the "Independents" rejoined the German Social-Democratic Party. p. 14

[7] See Lenin's article "What Should Not Be Imitated in the German Labour Movement" (*Selected Works,* Eng. ed., New York, 1943, Vol. IV, pp. 334-38). p. 19

[8] *Spartacists* — the members of the Spartacus League, formed during the First World War, in January 1916. At the beginning of the war the German Left Social-Democrats formed the "International" group led by Karl Liebknecht, Rosa Luxemburg, Franz Mehring, Clara Zetkin and others. It also called itself the "Spartacus League." The Spartacists

128

conducted revolutionary propaganda among the masses against the imperialist war and exposed the predatory policy of German imperialism and the treachery of the opportunist Social-Democratic leaders. But the Spartacists failed to free themselves of semi-Menshevik fallacies on cardinal questions of theory and policy. A criticism of the mistakes of the German Lefts is given in Lenin's "The Junius Pamphlet" (*Collected Works*, 4th Russ. ed., Vol. XXII, pp. 291-305), "A Caricature of Marxism and 'Imperialist Economism,' " (*ibid.*, Vol. XXIII, pp. 16-64) and other works, and in Stalin's letter to the editorial board of *Proletarskaya Revolutsia*, "Some Questions Concerning the History of Bolshevism" (*Works*, Eng. ed., Moscow, 1955, Vol. XIII, pp. 86-104). In 1917 the Spartacists affiliated to the Centrist Independent Social-Democratic Party of Germany, retaining their organizational independence within it. After the revolution in Germany in November 1918, they broke with the "Independents" and in December of the same year formed the Communist Party of Germany.

p. 19

[9] By Labourites Lenin meant the members of the British Labour Party, which was formed in 1900 as an affiliation of working-class organizations — trade unions and socialist parties and groups — for the purpose of securing the election of workers' representatives to parliament (hence its original name: Labour Representation Committee). It assumed the name of Labour Party in 1906. Extremely opportunistic, "bourgeois through and through" (Lenin), in its ideology and tactics, the Labour Party pursued a policy of class collaboration with the bourgeoisie. p. 23

[10] *Kerensky* — Prime Minister of the bourgeois Provisional Government of Russia which was overthrown by the Great October Socialist Revolution.

Kolchak and *Denikin* commanded the counter-revolutionary armies which, with the support of foreign intervention forces, waged civil war against the Soviet Republic. p. 25

[11] *Cadets* (Constitutional-Democratic Party) — the principal bourgeois party in Russia, the party of the liberal-monarchist bourgeoisie. It was founded in October 1905. Under the cloak of pseudo democracy and calling themselves the party of "people's freedom," the Cadets tried to win the peasantry to their side. They strove to preserve tsarism in the form of a constitutional monarchy. Subsequently, the Cadets became the party of the imperialist bourgeoisie. After the victory of the October Socialist Revolution, the Cadets organized counter-revolutionary conspiracies and revolts against the Soviet Republic. p. 25

[12] *Volapük* — an artificial language, devised by a south German, Johann Martin Schleyer in 1879. It did not gain popularity. p. 29

[13] *Dutch "Tribunists"* — the name given by Lenin to members of the Communist Party of Holland. The Tribunists originally made up the Left wing of the Social-Democratic Labour Party of Holland, taking their name from the newspaper *De Tribune*, founded in 1907. Expelled from the Social-Democratic Labour Party in 1909, they organized their own independent party, the Social-Democratic Party of Holland. The Tribunists represented the Left wing of the working-class movement in Holland but were never a consistently revolutionary party. In 1918 they took part in the formation of the Communist Party of Holland.   p. 29

[14] Horner, the pseudonym of Anton Panekoek.   p. 31

[15] *Kommunistische Arbeiterzeitung* — organ of a petty-bourgeois, anarcho-syndicalist group of "Left" Communists who broke away from the Communist Party of Germany (Spartacists) in 1919. The paper appeared from 1919 to 1927. The German "Left" Communists failed to carry out the decision of the Third Congress of the Communist International which called on them to abandon their sectarian tactics and join the Communist Party of Germany and were therefore expelled from the Communist International. Later the top leadership of the "Left" Communists degenerated into counter-revolutionaries.   p. 31

[16] *Trudoviki* — a group of petty-bourgeois democrats formed in April 1906 of peasant members of the first State Duma. The Trudoviki group existed in all four Dumas. During the world imperialist war of 1914-18 the Trudoviki took a chauvinist stand, and following the bourgeois-democratic revolution of February 1917, expressed the interests of the kulaks and sided with the counter-revolution.   p. 34

[17] The Party membership changed as follows in the period after the February Revolution of 1917 and up to the close of 1919: 80,000 at the time of the Seventh (April) All-Russian Conference of the R.S.D.L.P. (B.) in 1917; about 240,000 at the time of the Sixth R.S.D.L.P. (B.) Congress in July-August 1917; no less than 270,000 at the time of the Seventh R.C.P. (B.) Congress in March 1918, and 313,766 at the time of the Eighth R.C.P. (B.) Congress in March 1919.   p. 37

[18] V. I. Lenin, *Collected Works*, 4th Russ. ed., Vol. XXX, pp. 230-51.   p. 43

[19] See Karl Marx and Frederick Engels, *Selected Correspondence*, International Publishers, New York, 1942, pp. 115-16.   p. 44

[20] *Industrial Workers of the World (I.W.W.)* — an American labour organization founded in 1905. Its activities were marked by pronounced anarcho-syndicalist traits: it did not recognize the necessity of political struggle by the proletariat, denied the leading role of the proletarian

party, the need for an armed uprising to overthrow capitalism and the struggle for the dictatorship of the proletariat. The I.W.W. refused to work in the American Federation of Labour unions and subsequently degenerated into a sectarian anarcho-syndicalist group exerting no influence whatsoever on the workers. p. 46

[21] *The Italian Socialist Party* was founded in 1892 under the name of the Italian Workers' Party and renamed Italian Socialist Party in 1893. The Left wing gained strength following the October Socialist Revolution in Russia, and in January 1921, at the Livorno Congress, the Lefts broke with the party, convened a congress of their own and founded the Communist Party of Italy.

An influential Left wing developed within the Socialist Party during the years of fascist dictatorship, and in 1934 the party concluded an agreement on united action with the Communist Party of Italy. The agreement was the basis for co-operation between the two parties during and after the Second World War. A Right-wing group led by Saragat, which served the interest of American imperialism, withdrew from the Socialist Party in January 1947 and formed the Socialist Party of Italian Workers. p. 61

[22] The *Blanquists* were followers of the French revolutionary Louis Auguste Blanqui (1805-81). The classics of Marxism-Leninism, while regarding Blanqui as an outstanding revolutionary and adherent of socialism, criticized him for his sectarianism and conspiratorial methods of activity. "Blanquism," wrote Lenin, "is a theory that repudiates the class struggle. Blanquism expects that mankind will be emancipated from wage slavery, not by the class struggle of the proletariat, but through a conspiracy of a small minority of intellectuals" (see V. I. Lenin, "The Congress Summed Up," *Collected Works,* 4th Russ. ed., Vol. X, p. 360).
p. 62

[23] Frederick Engels, "Emigré Literature. II. The Program of the Blanquist Emigré from the Commune" (Karl Marx and Frederick Engels, *Collected Works,* Ger. ed., Berlin, Vol. XVIII, p. 533). p. 63

[24] Lenin is referring to the passage in Engels' letter to F. A. Sorge dated November 29, 1886, which criticizes the German Social-Democratic emigrants in America on the ground that for them theory "is a credo [creed] and not a guide to action" (Karl Marx and Frederick Engels, *Selected Correspondence,* International Publishers, New York, 1942, p. 450).
p. 68

[25] N. G. Chernyshevsky, *Selected Economic Writings,* Russ. ed., 1948, Vol. II, p. 550. p. 68

[26] *The British Socialist Party* was formed in 1911. It conducted Marxist propaganda and agitation and was described by Lenin as "not opportunist,"

and as *"really* independent of the Liberals." Its small membership and isolation from the masses lent the party a somewhat sectarian character.

During the first world imperialist war, two trends were revealed in the Party: one openly social-chauvinist, headed by Henry Hyndman, and the other internationalist, headed by Albert Inkpin and others. In April 1916 a split took place. Hyndman and his supporters found themselves in the minority and withdrew from the party. From that moment the internationalists assumed the leadership of the British Socialist Party, which later initiated the formation of the Communist Party of Great Britain in 1920. p. 77

[27] *The Socialist Labour Party* was organized in 1903 by a group of Left Social-Democrats who broke away from the Social-Democratic Federation. The *South Wales Socialist Society* — a small group made up predominantly of Welsh miners. The *Workers' Socialist Federation* — a small organization which grew out of the Women's Suffrage League and was made up mainly of women.

These "Left" organizations refused to join the Communist Party of Great Britain when it was founded (the inaugural congress was held on July 31-August 1, 1920), because its program included a clause calling for participation in parliamentary elections and affiliation to the Labour Party. The South Wales Socialist Society and the Workers' Socialist Federation (which had changed their names to Communist Labour Party and Communist Party respectively) merged with the Communist Party of Great Britain at the latter's congress in January 1921, and the party took the name of United Communist Party of Great Britain. The leadership of the Socialist Labour Party refused to join. p. 77

[28] *The Dreyfus case* — the framed-up trial organized in 1894 by the reactionary-royalist military clique in France against Dreyfus, a Jewish officer of the French General Staff. Dreyfus was sentenced to life imprisonment on false charges of espionage and high treason. The widespread public campaign for revision of the verdict was marked by a bitter struggle between the republicans and royalists and resulted in Dreyfus' acquittal in 1906. p. 103

[29] *The Kapp-Luttwitz putsch* — an attempt at a counter-revolutionary coup d'état in Germany, undertaken by Kapp, Luttwitz and other monarchists in March 1920. The plot was crushed within a few days thanks to the energetic action of the Berlin workers. p. 115

[30] *Augean stable* means a place marked by a staggering accumulation of corruption and filth. According to a Greek legend the stable of Augeas was left unclean for 30 years until Hercules cleaned it in one day. p. 117

[31] *"Soviet"* *"attorneys"* — collegiums of attorneys formed under the Soviets of Workers', Soldiers', Peasants' and Cossacks' Deputies in February 1918. They were abolished in October 1920. p. 123

列　宁
共产主义运动中的"左派"幼稚病

＊

外文出版社出版（北京）
1965年（32开）第一版
1970年第二次印刷
编号：（英）1050—368
00061
1/1—E—741P

㉑